the women of Advent

a gathering of scattered hearts, past and present

all text and art
by Sheila Atchley
all photography by Sheila Atchley
unless otherwise noted

In my dreams,
we are, each of us,
gathered right here.

Here we are, bringing our scattered
fragments, so they can be gathered up
and made into 12 baskets of blessing...

contents

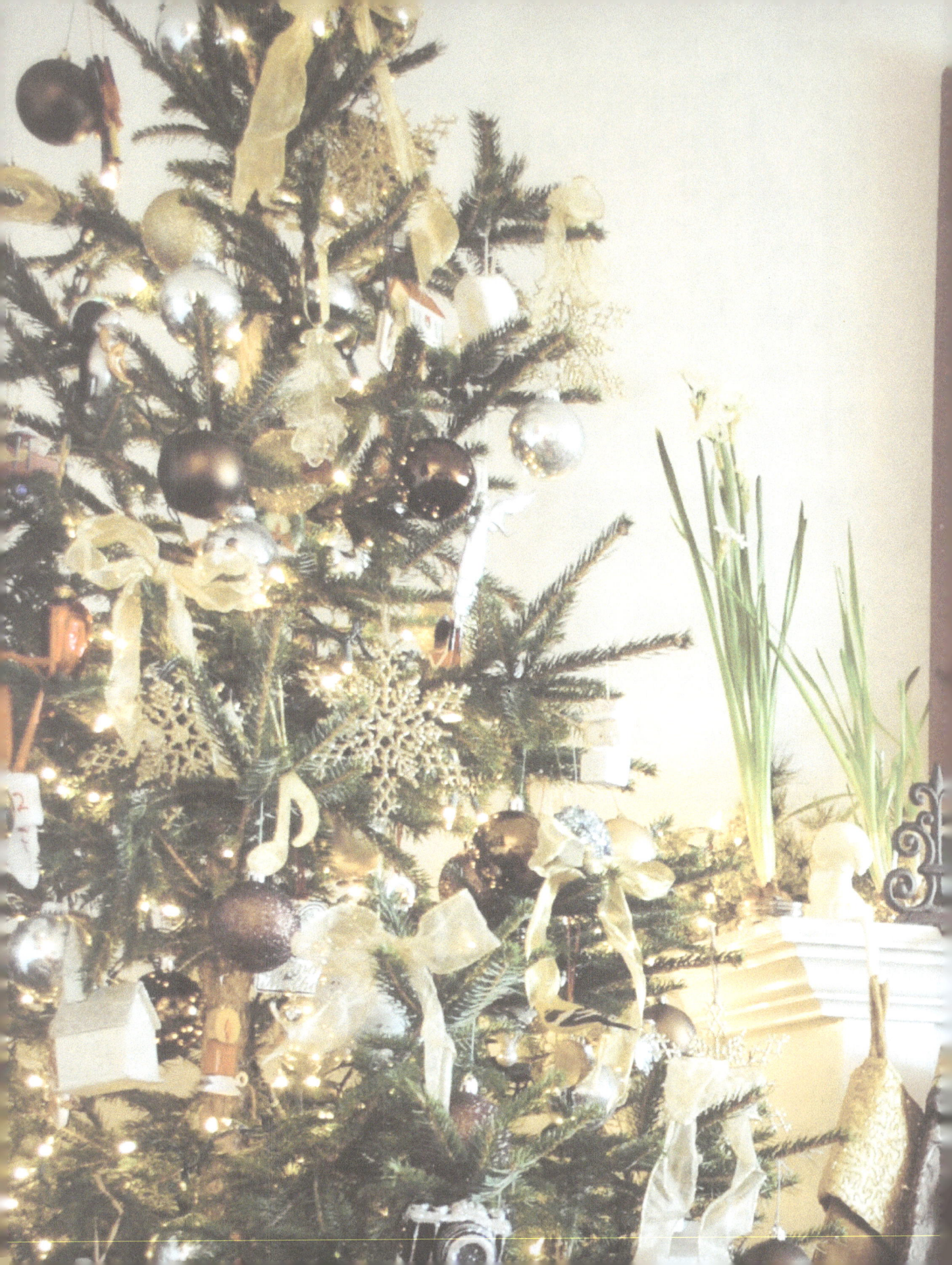

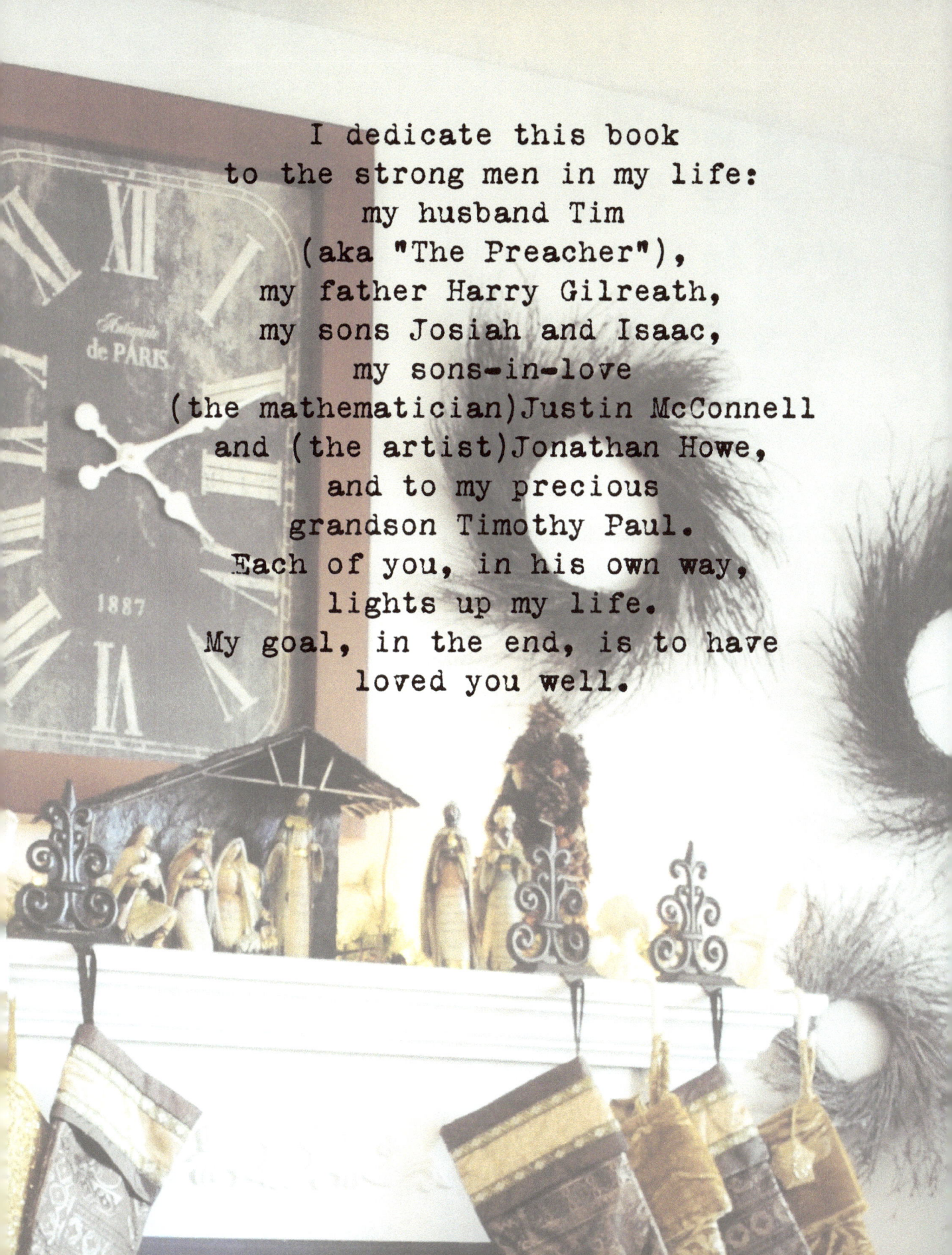

I dedicate this book
to the strong men in my life:
my husband Tim
(aka "The Preacher"),
my father Harry Gilreath,
my sons Josiah and Isaac,
my sons-in-love
(the mathematician)Justin McConnell
and (the artist)Jonathan Howe,
and to my precious
grandson Timothy Paul.
Each of you, in his own way,
lights up my life.
My goal, in the end, is to have
loved you well.

You are holding my very first book.

Thank you.

I can't thank you enough, in fact, but I probably should introduce myself first.
My name is Sheila Atchley, and I am an artist, a preacher's wife, an empty nester,
an ordinary mom to four extraordinary adults,
and an imperfect Mimi to four perfect wildlings.

I am a flagrant creative who is madly in love with written words and spoken words and
the Word made flesh, who dwelt among humans.

Thanks in advance for grace, as I alone have both written and edited what you are about
to read.

I am a woman who, in recent months and years
has felt deeply scattered.

In fact, if I were to choose one word that best describes how I feel,
it would be that one word: scattered.

Menopause does evil things to one's attention span. Just sayin'. I can't even.

I am fairly certain all women, of all ages, and in all seasons are feeling me right this
minute. We feel so scattered.

I'm grateful for all the women in my life,
and especially in my own family,
who understand what it is to be completely scattered and undone,
yet we love each other through it, and in spite of it

And I am grateful for you, dear reader.

Frankly, I'm delighted to even be able to (finally!) type the words "dear reader".
I keep having to pinch myself, and encourage myself time and again that

"...this isn't a blog post. This isn't a blog post. This isn't a blog post. This isn't..."

This is a book! This is an exploration of the lives of the women listed in the genealogy of Jesus, as found in Matthew chapter 1. I can never open the New Testament, I can never touch the page of Matthew 1, without hearing the "Hallelujah Chorus" in my head. It's always Christmas, there in Matthew 1. The grace of God is on display in the lives of ordinary women, living their ordinary lives, having ordinary Wednesdays. (I can't use the term "ordinary Tuesday". It's taken. And besides - it really is Wednesday, as I write this.) Are you ready? Are you ready to bring your scattered heart and your scattered attention and your scattered finances and your scattered laundry and your scattered plans to a good...great...gathering God?

These are the stories of the sorority of the scattered-and-gathered.
This is your story, too.

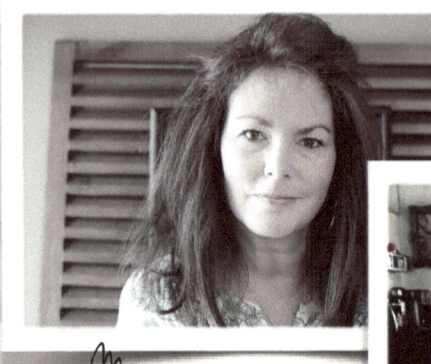

Me

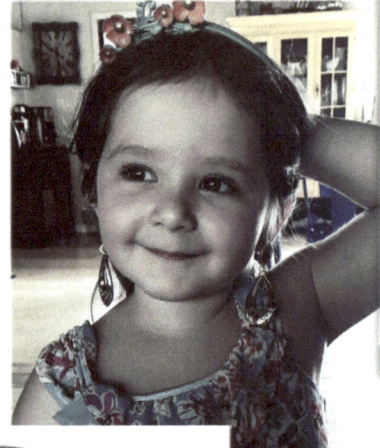

grand-girl
Aidyn Esther

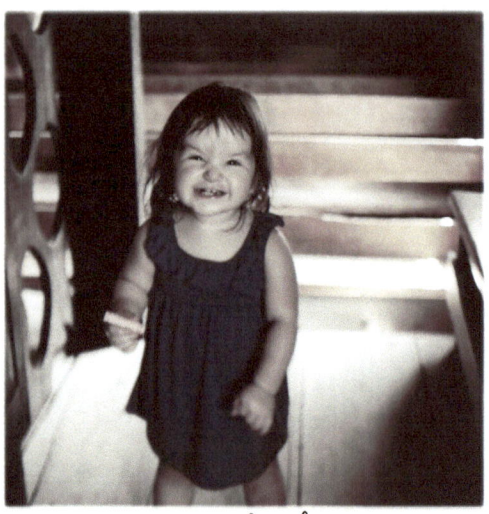

grand-girl
Susanna Joy

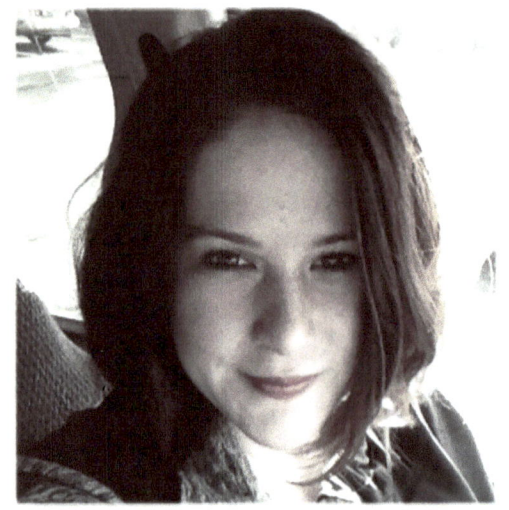

daughter Hannah - mama of
Timothy Paul
(she has an identical twin)

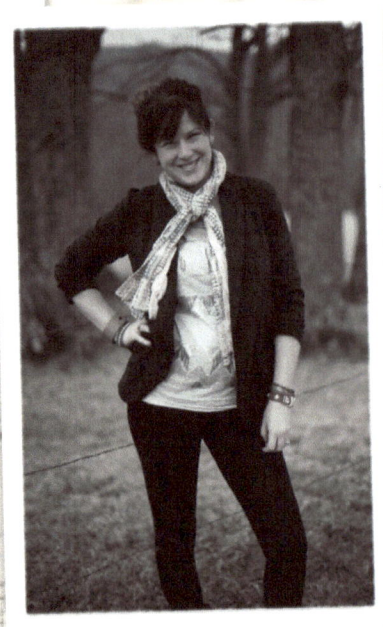

daughter Sarah - mama of
Aidyn and Susanna

I love to honor
the girls and women in my life...

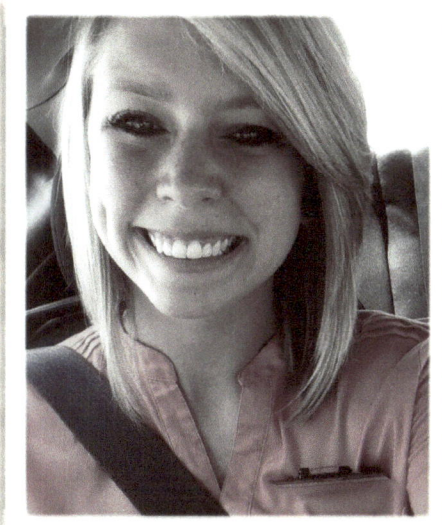

Christine - mama of Avery

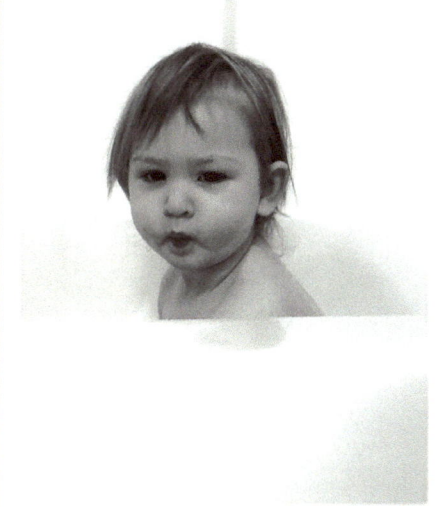

grand-girl Avery Christine

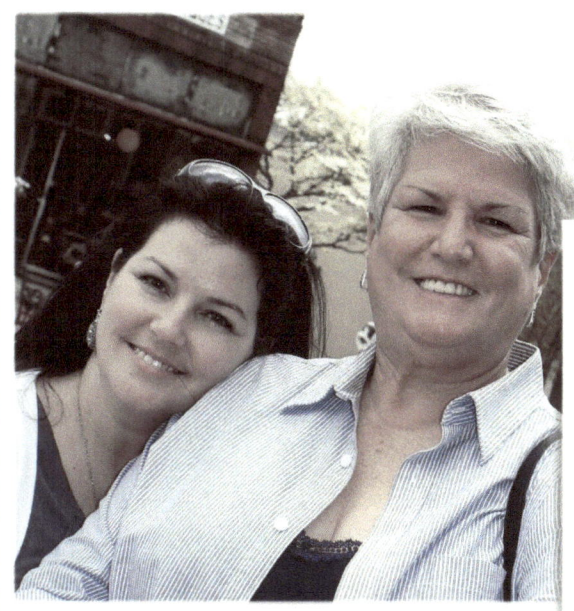

my sister Lynn - mama of Erica
and my mother Sue - mama of my sister and me

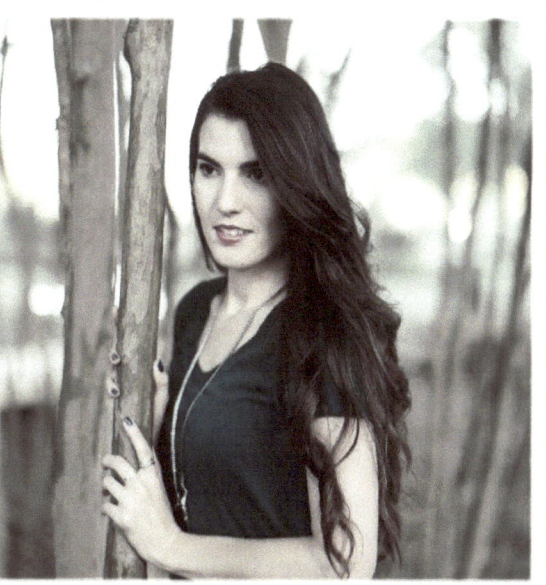

my niece Erica

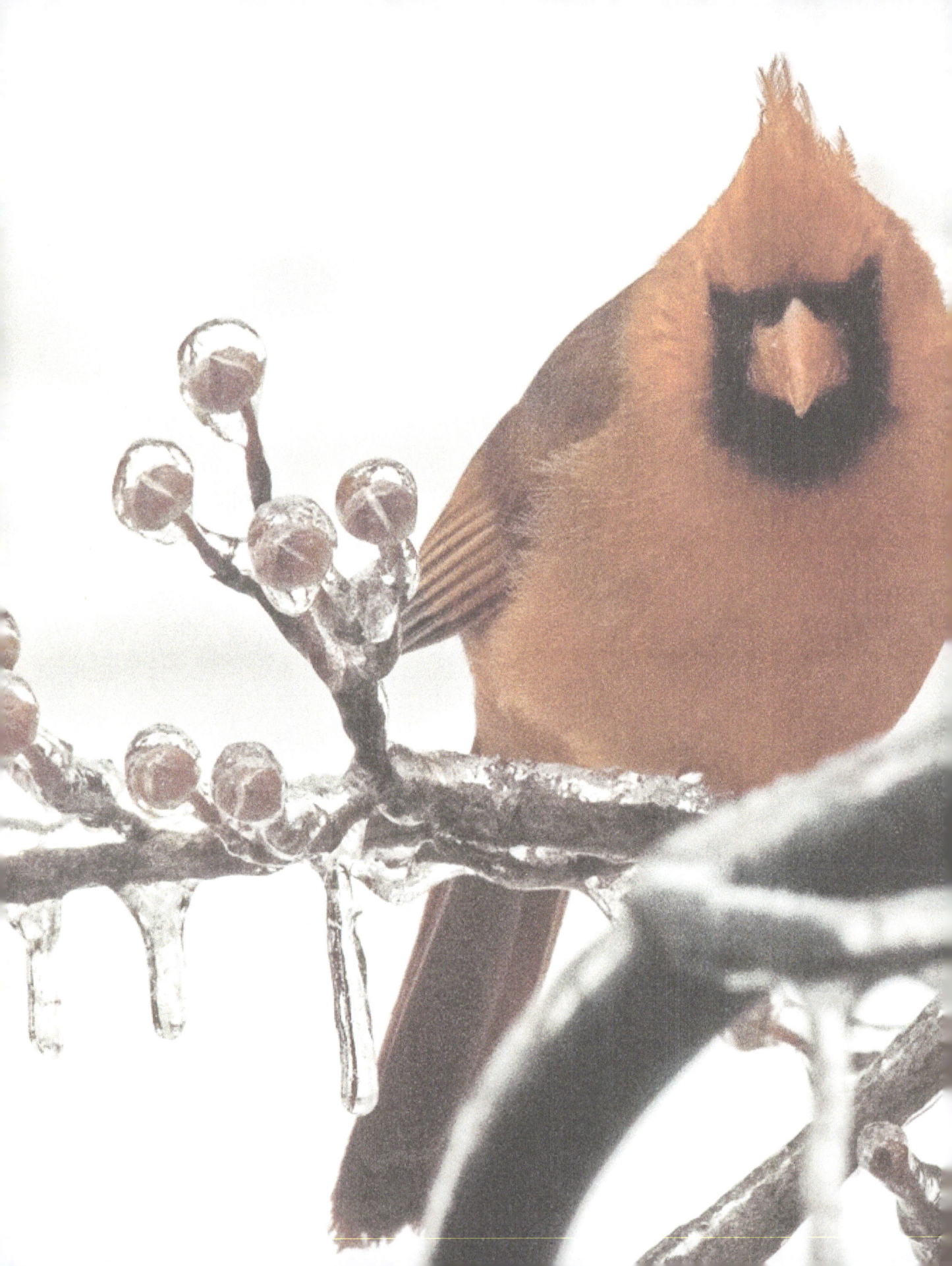

week one

Tamar
"SHE IS MORE RIGHTEOUS THAN I.."

and

Rehab
(THE. HARLOT.)

...far from being a "bad girl of the Bible", Tamar was the only woman in the old testament to be declared righteous in her day. On the other hand, Rehab can legitimately be thought of as a "bad girl", but that just makes us love her more. This week, we read how our God inserts marginalized women into His own ancestry. These women are going to amaze us.

this page's photography by Tim Atchley

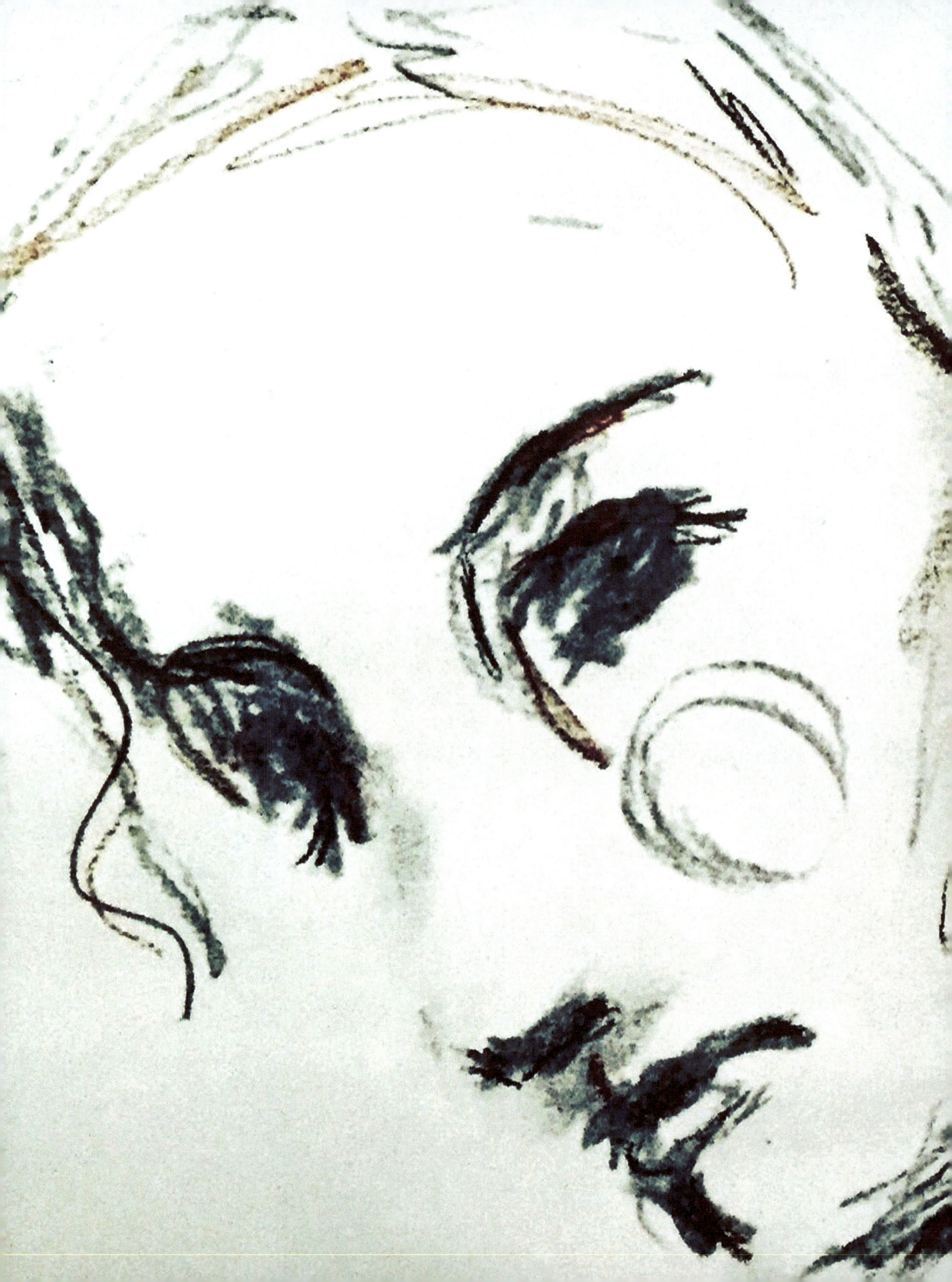

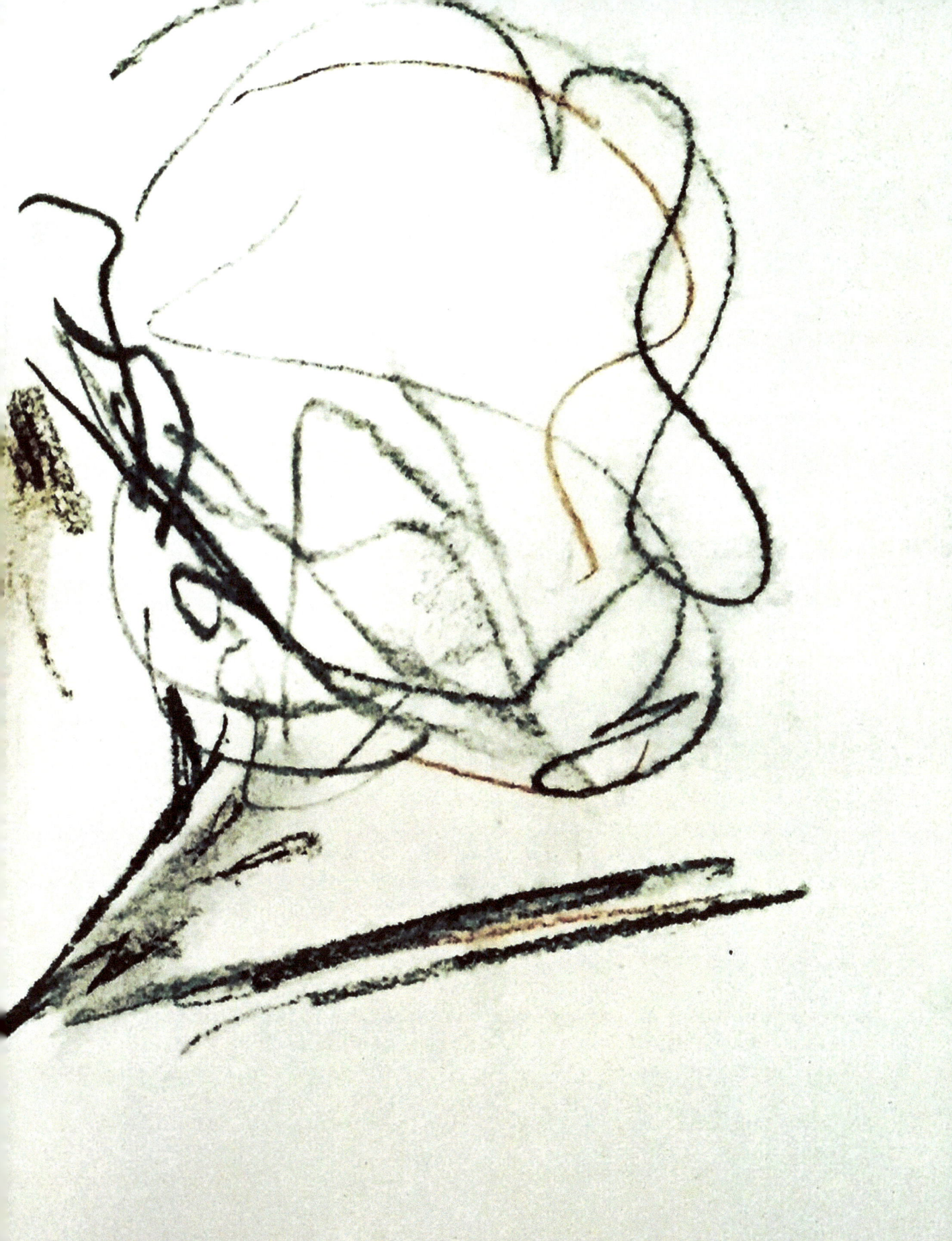

In ancient times, two things determined your sense of belonging in the world: your pedigree and your gender. Your gender determined whether you had any voice in the events of your life. Your pedigree in those days served the same purpose that your resume serves today. If your nationality was right, if your family tree contained the right names, you had the respect necessary to succeed - in much the same way that the right education, followed by the right series of jobs supposedly ensures the same respect today.

No one controls the gender of their own birth, and no one chooses family they are born into.

This is the story of Tamar, the first of five women mentioned in the genealogy of Jesus. The preaching and teaching of Tamar seems to be held in almost customary low esteem. Few Bible teachers ever dedicate an entire message to her.

I aim to challenge the unfortunate inclination to ignore Tamar, and all seemingly insignificant women, for that matter. There is no such thing as an unimportant woman.

At first glance, Tamar is the ultimate symbol of a powerless woman. She was "taken" by Judah, Scripture says, in order to bear children for Judah's oldest son Er. Tamar was likely given in exchange for animals or physical goods. Tamar's mother is forever nameless in Scripture. She was most likely bargained for as well, when she was Tamar's age, with her having had no voice in the exchange, as though she were a fine cloak or a goat. Tamar is taken in the same manner.

But we do know one thing about Tamar's mother.

We know the name she gave her daughter. While sons were given names by the father, often a daughter's name was left to the mother to decide.

The meaning of Tamar's name is "palm tree", an ancient symbol of fertility.

It's all we need to know. By this, we know that Tamar's mother
never hoped for anything more for her daughter than what she
herself had only ever been. All her hopes, dreams, and
blessings for Tamar were contained within her name: that she
would never be barren.

Tamar-the-little-girl, had no one. . .ever. . .to tell her she
could do anything other than to become a man's property, and if
she was blessed, to give him a son. So she never dreamed of
anything else, she never hoped for anything more than that.
The value of her entire life, and her whole sense of belonging,
of being gathered in, part of a family and part of society, her
whole sense of being at all chosen and special, was forever
fused to having a husband and bearing children. If this were
not true merely by virtue of the prevailing culture, it surely
became true by virtue of her name. The best blessing her
nameless mother could confer upon her was the blessing of her
name: fertile.

In modern terms, if I had no other ambitions for my daughter
than for her to be fertile and make babies, I might name her
"Bunny". That's just the reality we are dealing with here in
Scripture, and we may as well understand it without judging it
by our enlightened standards. Our judgements get in the way of
our correct interpretation. The treatment of girls and women
as property was never in the heart of God, but it was the
prevailing and fully accepted custom of ancient times. "It was
what it was", so to speak.

Genesis 38 is an independent unit, a cut-away story, it is the
"aside" between Genesis 37 and 39. Please do read it. This
chapter 38 presents us with an abrupt change of tone. It is as
if the Holy Spirit wants us to understand that we are about to
hear an incredibly important, astonishingly interesting, and
fabulously scandalous story - complete with a beginning,
middle, and end. Verse one opens with, "And it came to pass at
that time…"

We see words like "in the process of time", and "it came to
pass", repeated over and over in the story. The narrative ends
in verse 30 with the words, "and afterward…"

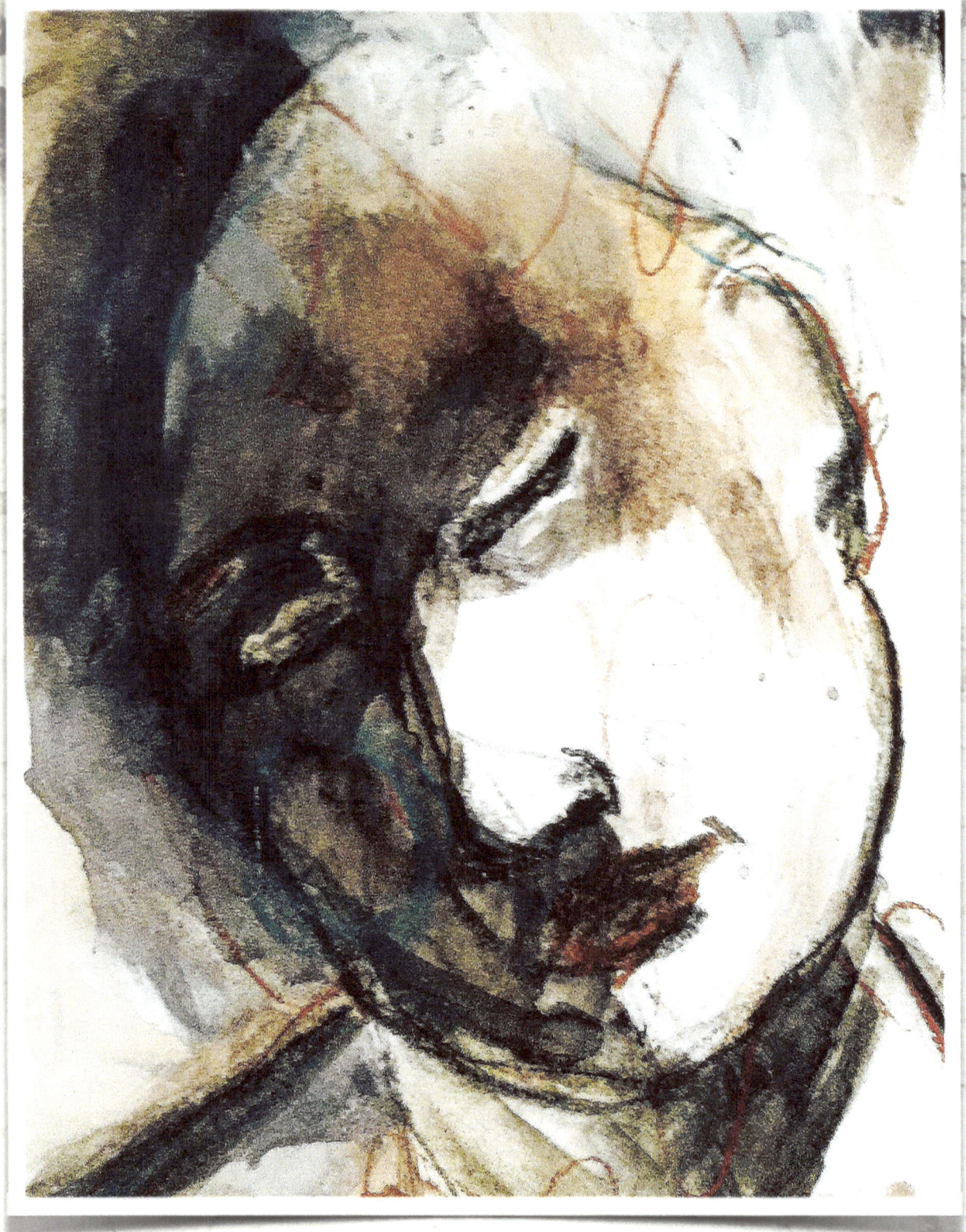

"Tamar"
Rendered in charcoal and watercolor,
with oil pastel accents of color.

There are seven characters introduced in the first paragraph, including Judah, Tamar, and three of Judah's sons, Er, Onan, and Shelah, in order of birth. The first two sons became Tamar's husbands in succession, and we find both of them are dead by verse 10.

After the death of the eldest son, Er, Judah ordered his second son Onan to "go into his brother's wife and perform the duty of raising up offspring for his deceased brother."

Once again, we have to refrain from using our modern, enlightened sensibilities as a template for interpreting Scripture. If it were me, today, and my pastor-husband died, and I was forced to become the wife of one of his four brothers, I would be driven to disfigure my face with my own fork, to put it bluntly. But that's getting into family dynamics that are best left alone.

It is important to understand that this custom (which later became part of the Jewish civil laws) was one of the few rules that fell completely in the interests of the woman. Without sons, a woman had no family and no means of support. A childless widow was one of the most vulnerable members of society, doomed to poverty and abuse. A son would inherit his father's name and the portion of his father's estate. It was understood that the son would then take care of his mother. Had Tamar become pregnant with either of the first two son's child, Judah would have been happy to enfold her into the family's estate. She would have been cared for always, in that way.

This important rule and custom was a cherished right of the widowed woman. It was in no way something she resented, or felt victimized by. The widow, if deprived of this right, could appeal to the elders, and the one (whether that be father-in-law, or brother-in-law) who failed his responsibility would be publicly shamed. And in that culture, to be openly shamed was almost as severe a punishment as death to a man.

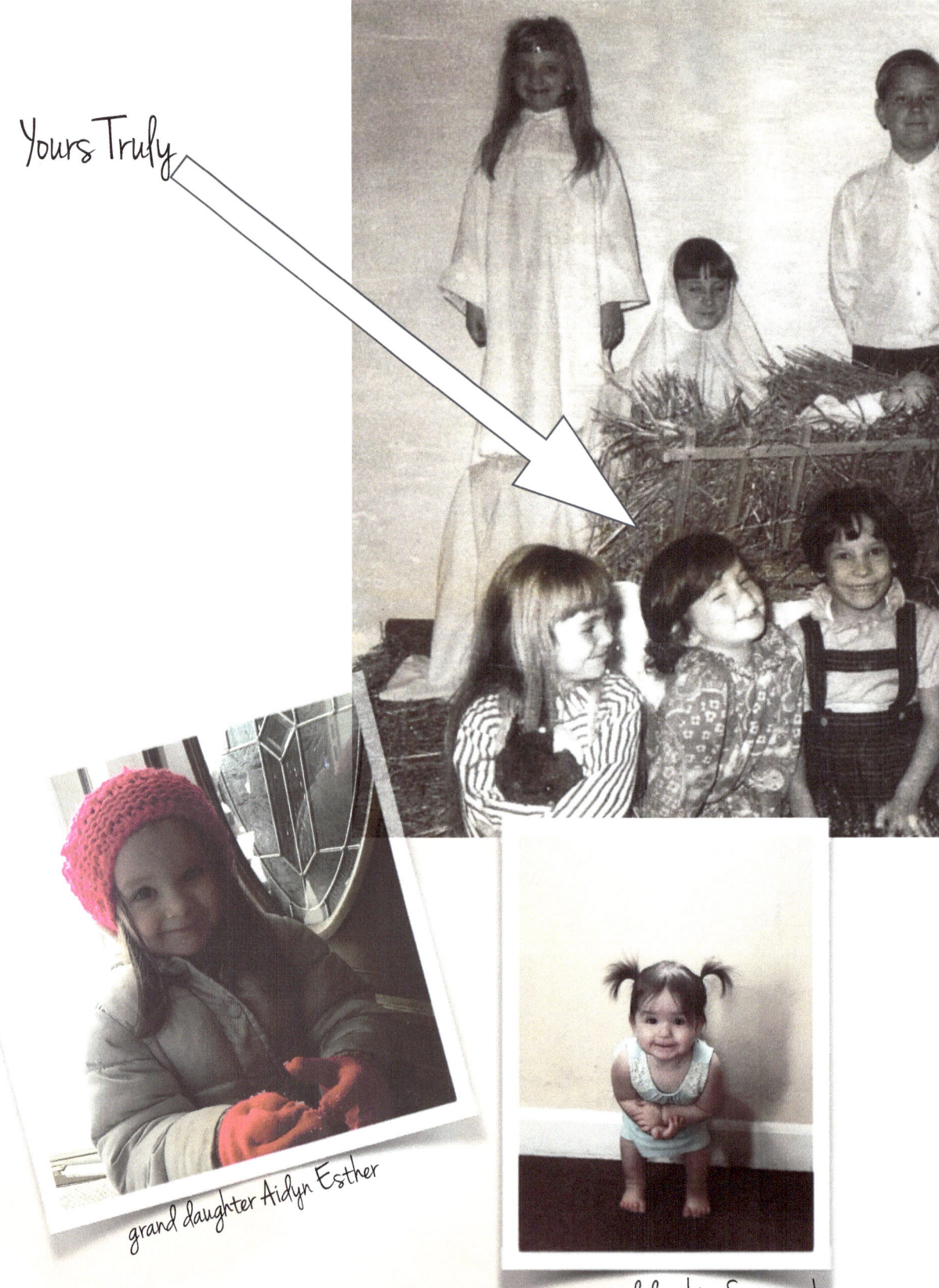

Yours Truly

grand daughter Aidyn Esther

grand daughter Susanna Joy

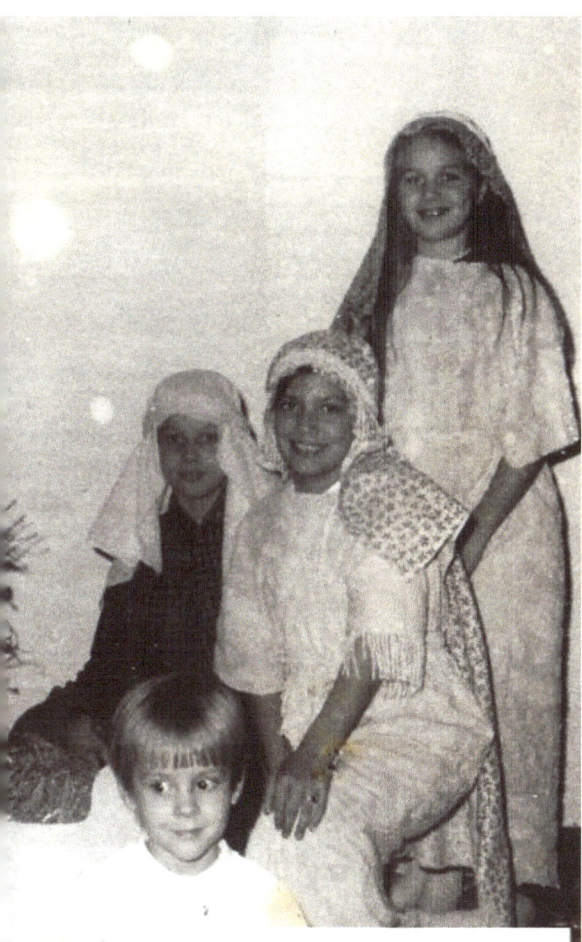

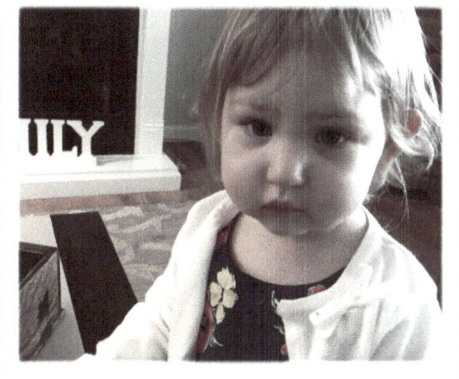

grand daughter Avery Christine

Any time I do a character study
of a woman in Scripture,
I always try to imagine her in
each and every season of her life.

The little girl becomes the woman.

For reasons that are not quite clear
to me now,
I had a very troubled childhood.
I wet the bed every night from about age 4 to
age 13. I felt terrible fear.
I even heard voices, and often
wondered what it would be like to harm myself.

Then, one day I experienced the overwhelming
supernatural presence of God.
I had a visitation.
Every fear I had at the time, left instantly.
I slept that night for the first time I could
remember, without hearing voices.

I pray that my grand=girls grow up
knowing the love of God for them.
I pray they, too, have supernatural
encounters with God.
May our little ones know the
manifest presence of God,
and feel fully loved
each and every day of their lives.

So the two older sons both married Tamar in succession. The
first one dies, then the second son uses her for his pleasure,
while being most unwilling to dilute his own inheritance by
raising up offspring for his brother. Both older sons
displeased the Lord, and ended up dead. Judah was inwardly
convinced that it was Tamar's fault. It was conventional
belief that certain women of unholy, mystical power could deal
out death to their husbands.

Tamar was innocent, yet Judah sends her away. She was sent
away a widow, yet somehow still betrothed to yet another
husband - Judah's youngest (an obligation which Judah has no
intention of ever fulfilling). She was unloved by any man,
ever, and unable to marry anyone else, even should another man
want her. She was tossed away as a homeless daughter,
belonging nowhere. An outcast in the family into which she
married, she was also a barren and childless shame to the
parents who named her "fertile".

And all of it, likely before her twentieth birthday.
All of it, out of her control. Judah was a double-dealing
deceiver, who had no concern for Tamar, basically conferring
the status of non-entity to her by ordering her to stay home
until Shelah grows up, while having no intention of giving him
to her to obtain children by, and thus be part of the tribe of
Judah again.

"It came to pass" - after some time goes by, the story develops
further. Tamar has long since been sent back home, Shelah is
of age to marry and procreate (likely being only a year or so
behind Onan), yet nothing is happening. Judah's wife dies, and
Judah spends the required time "in mourning", that is to say,
in abstinence. Now that time was over, and it happened to
coincide with the festival of sheep shearing - a time when
people feasted and drank wine and relaxed. Tamar had somehow
heard the news of Judah's wife passing, and of Judah's
traveling to the village of Timnah for the sheep-shearing
festival.

She also now understands what was in the mind of Judah when he sent her away. She knows she cannot trust Judah, and she takes massive action to save herself by recovering her status as a child bearing member of the tribe of Judah. The story develops quickly from here, with a series of sweeping action words. And this is the point at which many a well-meaning moralist becomes scandalized; because Tamar disguises herself by simply putting off her widow's clothing, putting on different robes, and, carefully veiling her face, she goes out to intercept Judah...

...with the intent to unwittingly seduce him.

What we have to keep in the front of our mind, is that Tamar is asserting a right. Her means are questionable, but her strong sense of family responsibility is stellar. She simply <u>both</u> will not allow Judah to risk having no heritage (having lost two sons already), <u>and</u> she will not allow herself to live as a powerless, marginalized non-entity without her right to patriarchal protection.

The Bible says Tamar "saw" that Shelah had grown up, yet she had not been given to him in marriage. She saw truth without using her physical sight. Tamar perceived.
Yet Judah failed to perceive his own daughter-in-law, though he saw her with his physical eyes. He saw her physically, but failed to <u>recognize</u>. Ah, but each one of us fails in the same way, when "seeing we do not see and hearing we do not hear". It isn't enough to see. Only when what we see becomes what we rightly perceive and recognize, do we actually possess wisdom.

It is a tragic wonder to me that Judah was so uncaring as to fail to recognize his own daughter-in-law - because he failed to <u>see</u> her, all along, with the eyes of his heart. He failed to know her, to want to truly "see" her (and don't we all need to be seen!), because he failed to value her, however short the time of their near-relationship might have been.

How important is it to "see" someone — however removed from our inner circle, but especially those in our inner circle? How life-giving is it to be seen? Being seen is destiny-altering. Being recognized, spiritually, is deeply connected to our sense of well being. We need someone to mirror to us how God sees us. We need to know who heaven says we are. When our need to be seen is met, we need not resort to veils and masks to get attention. We are loved, as we are.

Tamar, being unseen, must gain attention and claim her rights in the only way available to her. The only way to recover her place in the household was to appeal to Judah's appetites, and conceive his child. It should be noted that, even under what was the then-custom, in remote cases like this, Judah would not have been stoned or put to death for the crime of incest. Judah was an unwitting partner to Tamar, to be certain. But under the custom of the day, though it was undesirable and quite uncommon for the generations to be secured this way, everyone would have looked the other way, particularly if there was no other way. Judah would have been in no danger of drastic repercussion.

But Judah was obviously not at all intending to give his youngest son to Tamar, much less was he ever going to willingly perform the "family duty" to the widow himself. Thus, we see that the initiative is taken by Tamar, from beginning to end. She changes her apparel, she sits where she will be seen (and taken for a prostitute, which she was not), and she proves to be a shrewd negotiator of terms.

Judah does was Tamar knows he will do. Judah, caught up in the spirit of festival, and fresh from a time of mourning and abstinence, is low on self control. He solicits her for sex, and she quickly sets the terms. The conversation is brief and lucid. Tamar would have made an amazing double-agent. She completes her mission flawlessly, and Judah is never the wiser. He exchanges his own seal and staff, upon Tamar's demand, as a deposit for services rendered, until he can bring her the final payment of a goat…

...which makes me both laugh and cry. Because it was Judah who got the idea to sell his brother Joseph, in the previous chapter. He deceived his stricken father with a robe dipped in the blood of a. . .goat. Now it is he who is being deceived by a woman's veil, and his own hasty promise of a goat. Yet, in contrast to Judah's haste and lack of forethought, all of Tamar's actions are well-planned and even more well executed. Her ruse is businesslike and precise, and once accomplished, Tamar quickly changes back into her widow's garb once again.

Verse 20 opens a new scene. Judah asks a friend to deliver the goat, and retrieve his seal and staff - to save himself the shame and embarrassment of collecting them himself. When his friend couldn't find the mystery woman, Judah stops looking for her - again, to save face. The final part of this story then unfolds as a climax, when Judah and Tamar confront one another in a most unexpected way.

The faith of Tamar is nothing short of audacious. She takes uncommon initiative, believing it was possible that somehow she will conceive a baby and secure her entire future, based on a "one night stand". I get the sense that she took this plan of hers one step at a time, one day at a time. There was no way she could know immediately whether her plan was a success, or if it was for naught, or what would happen to her when she did conceive. No one was there to tell her that it would all work out. She hadn't read Genesis 38, to see what the outcome of her story would be.

She lived her story exactly as we live our own: one hour, one minute, one day at a time. She took initiative and responsibility for her life without any guarantee of the desired outcome. As should you and I, my friend.

No one would have blamed her for living life with a learned helplessness. No one was offering her savvy solutions. She couldn't google "how to increase your chances of conception", and get a few ideas. She couldn't sue or claim disability. She couldn't take an online class entitled "Leadership and Moxie for Widows".

Yet, her moxie was <u>epic.</u>

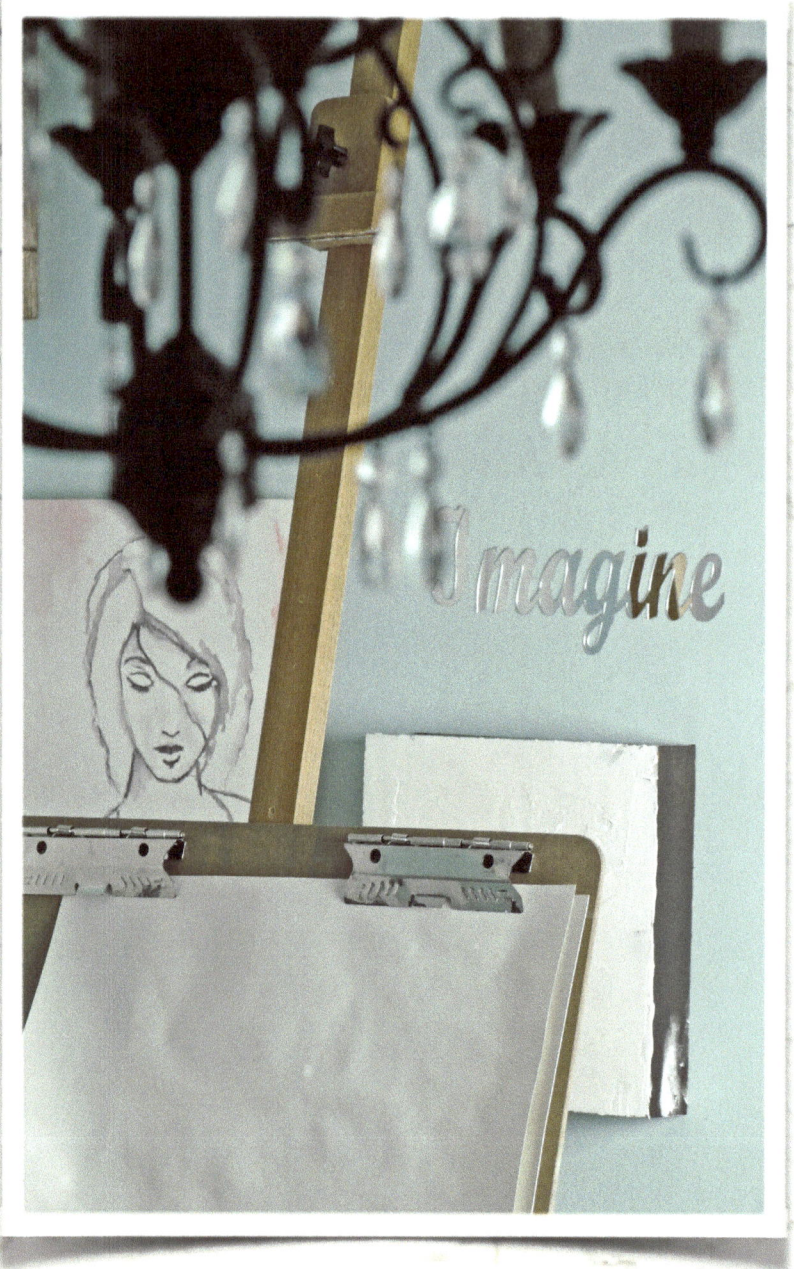

"On the Easel"
I keep several large clipboards atop the various
easels in my studio. On these, I keep
finished pieces (rendered on paper)
and works in progress...

Tamar's pregnancy becomes obvious at only three months, and in spite of Tamar's long widow's robes (we soon find out why). Judah was informed of it, and his all-too-rash response was to command that she be brought forth and burned as a harlot. The sexual double-standard of Judah is egregious and absurd. And again, the impetuous behavior of Judah is contrasted with the cautious and calculating actions of Tamar.

Tamar could not defend herself, nor could she hire anyone else to defend her, yet Judah's judgements were as legally binding on her as the verdict of any modern court of law. Justice was denied her. Incapable of initiating any legal proceedings, she simply delivered a message to Judah. She dared not speak to him directly, because he was already provoked. Tamar, in her wisdom, knew she needed him to consider her case calmly.

Tamar presented Judah with the items that belonged to him. The syntax in the original Hebrew indicates a sure and definite pause in the narrative. We will never know whether Judah stopped in his tracks upon the sight of what was in Tamar's hands, or if Tamar took a deep breath before gasping out the words, "Recognize." Unbeknownst to either of them, all of human history, and the lineage of God-in-flesh hung in the balance in that moment of silence. Scripture indicates a significant moment of suspended animation. Silence.

{a very "pregnant pause"} "Recognize whose these are, the seal with the cord and the staff!"

Recognize. It is the same Hebrew word used when Judah's father was presented with the bloody robes of Joseph, and asked to "... recognize whether this be thy son's coat or not."

This man, who asked his own father to "recognize" what was in fact his deception, this man who could not recognize his own daughter-in-law, was brought to a decisive and historic reckoning. For the first time, he both saw and perceived. He was handed his own seal and staff and asked to recognize to whom they belonged, and told that man was the father of the baby Tamar held in her womb.

Judah's response reverberates through time, down to us today: "She hath been more righteous than I."

Some translations say, "She is in the right, and I am wrong." This particular word in Hebrew for "righteous" is the feminine form of the verb to "be righteous" (tsadqah), and is a unique occurrence in all of Scripture. Thus, after recognizing the objects placed before him, after recognizing his deep culpability in Tamar's desperate situation, Judah utters his final words in this story: "She hath been more righteous (tsadqah) than I; because I gave her not to Shelah my son."

The stunning revelation is that Tamar is the only woman in all of old covenant scripture to be declared righteous in her day. So, toss out every message you've heard or book you've read that portrays Tamar as one of the "bad girls" of the Bible. Because, if you read carefully, even when she changed clothes and veiled herself, sitting in the gate of the city, the text says, "When Judah saw her, he thought her to be a harlot." The text never even says that Tamar dressed like a harlot. She changed clothes and put on a veil. Then she sat where harlots often sat.

Yes, deception is wrong. But Judah's own words are referencing not so much ownership of sexual sin, because culturally, he simply wasn't culpable. His words were ownership of his own deception. He never intended to give his youngest son to Tamar. He explicitly states that his sin of deception was worse than hers.

Of course, incest is one of the worst sins we can imagine. But the custom of the day would have exonerated Judah, had he no other option but to continue the bloodline through Tamar. Judah never knew he slept with Tamar, Scripture is quite clear. So Judah is not guilty of incest - but he is guilty of violating his relationship with Tamar, and reneging on his responsibility to give her provision and protection as a member of his household.

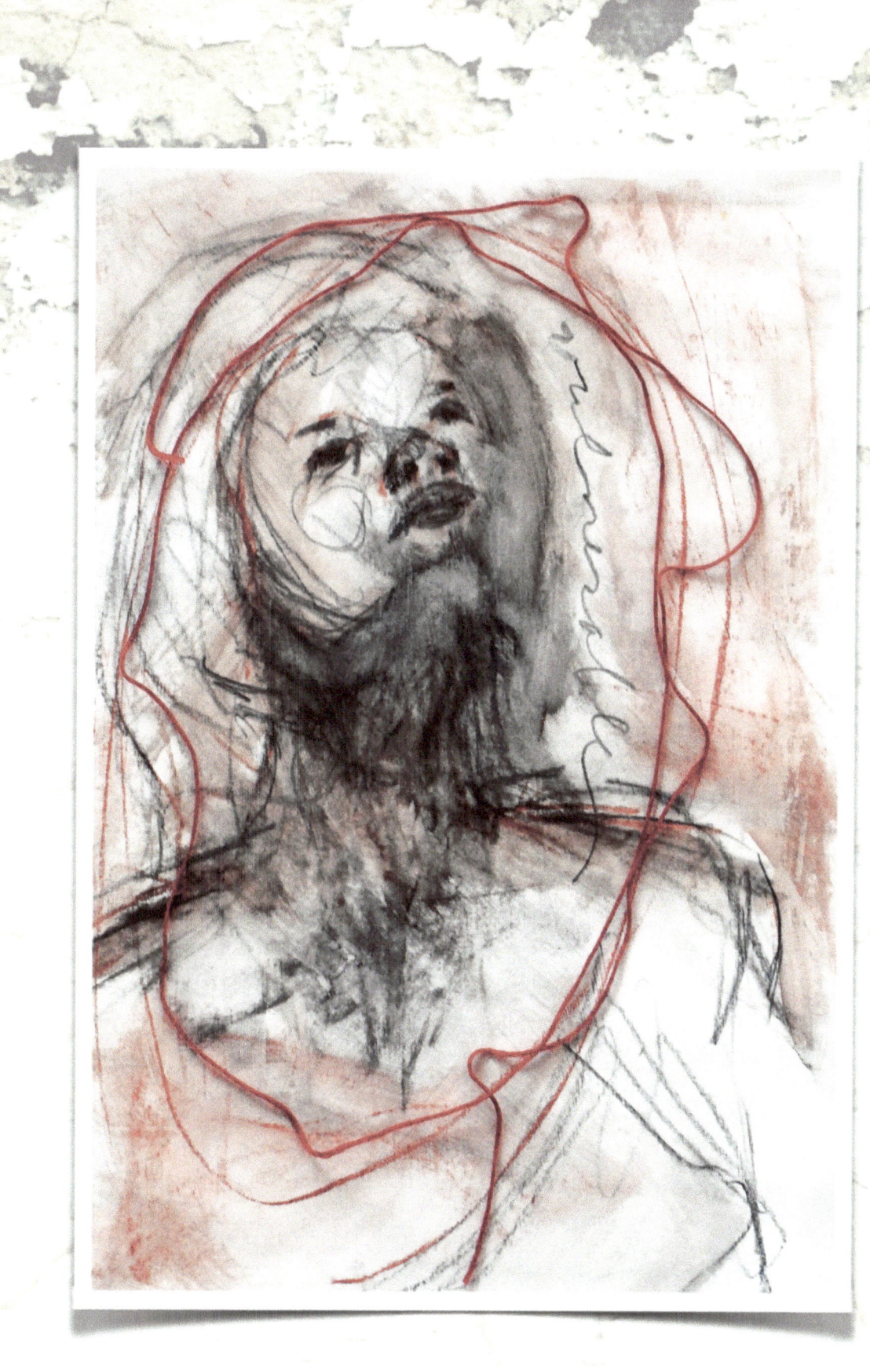

Tamar is actually being portrayed as taking initiative to claim what should have been hers all along - ever since she was taken from her family to marry Er. This story is, in fact, one of the best #truestory illustrations of how the sovereignty of God and the initiative of a woman work together to accomplish what was God's idea all along.

God was establishing the genealogy of Himself through the initiative of a woman who lived in the cultural margins. Make no mistake, He is still doing it today.
He is still telling His story through the lives of women in the cultural margins - women who live in sketchy neighborhoods, women who are lower-middle-class white, women who are impoverished black or Hispanic, women who have been abused and overlooked. When you see them, don't count them out. Rather, call out what you know is in them - Divine Destiny.

We can be for one another what Tamar never had. She never had one single soul to encourage her to seize the day. We can do that for each other. We can call one another to take holy initiative; we can inspire another woman to take her rightful place in history for the glory of God.

The closing paragraph in Genesis 38 offers us another surprise, as the story ends. Not only did God grant Tamar conception, not only did He give her a son. . .

. . .He granted her two sons. Twin boys. This was the ultimate stamp of favor and, dare I say it? Approval. Tamar carried two baby boys to term, no small thing in her day; she was able to give birth to them without dying in childbirth herself, and they both were healthy. The story of their birth closely mirrors their grandfather's birth story in Genesis 25. Tamar named one of her sons "Perez". Perez became an ancestor to David, who was an ancestor to God.

Perez means "breakthrough". God's sovereignty, working together with a woman's initiative, creates breakthrough in this world still today. Tamar is such a picture of the grace of God. Here was a woman whose mother was nameless, but her name will be remembered always. Here was a woman who resorted to devious means, but from a heart that beat with a passion to continue the family name.

Friends, some of my worst antics have stemmed out of a passion for the same. My heart is zealous for the church – and I have resorted to desperate efforts, made in my flesh, attempting to convince people to value the bride of Jesus the way Jesus values her. So this message of grace gives me hope. People indeed may look on the outward appearance of things, but God really does look at the heart.

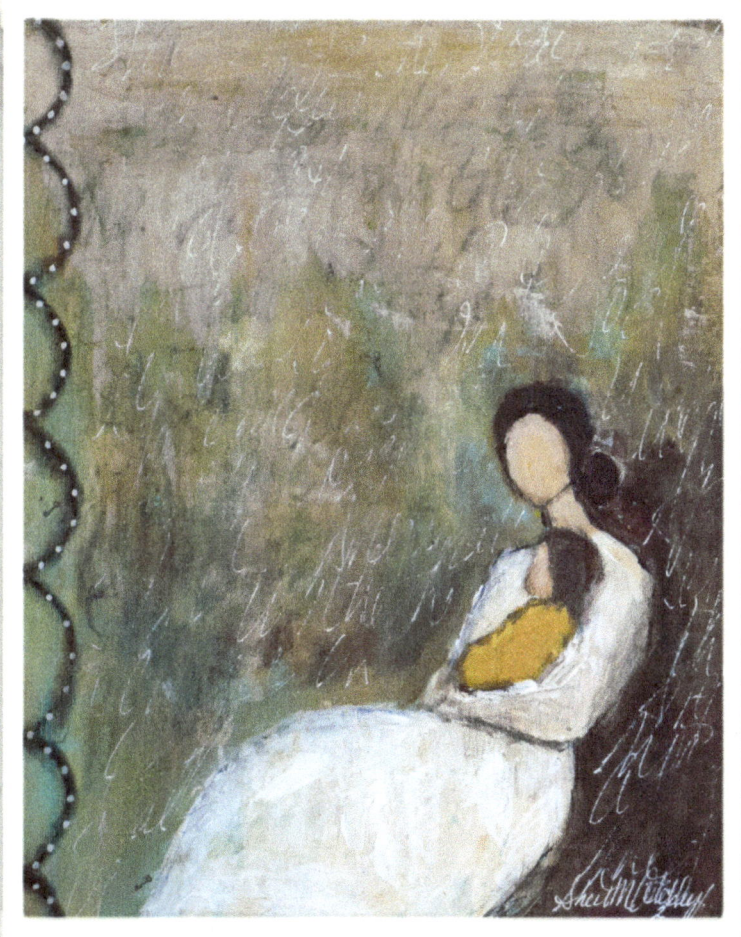

"The Mother"

A mixed media on canvas, rendered in acrylics, charcoal, willow stick, ink, and oil pastel.

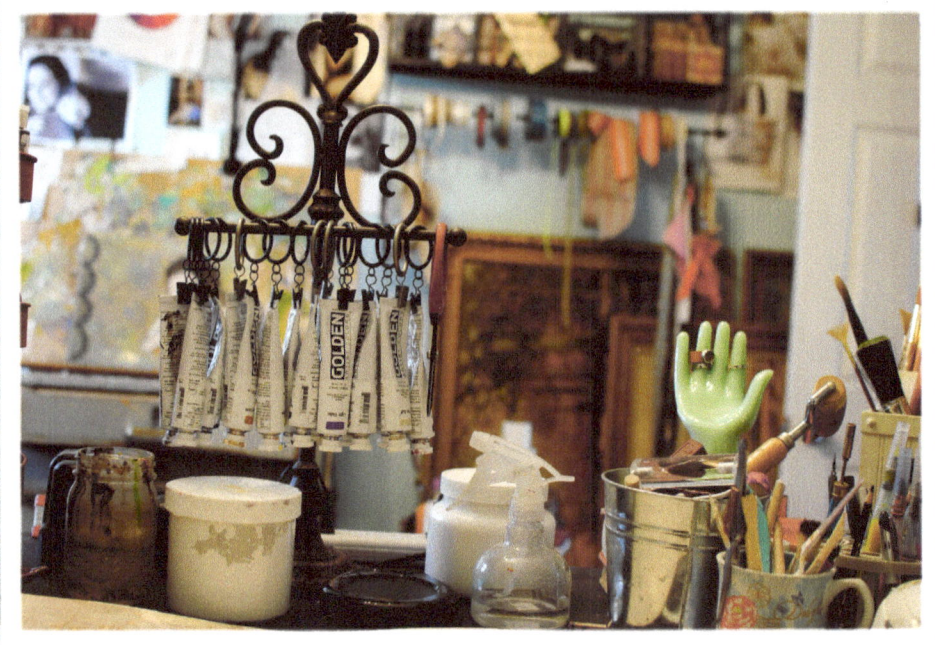

This is how I keep my tube paints handy.
I picked up a metal stand meant for bathroom hand towels,
then clipped inexpensive curtain clips (from the dollar store)
to the end of each tube of paint.
Works like a charm . . .

I also have a
cute little wall
easel for the
grand-wildlings.

They love to come in
and doodle on it, when
I am working.

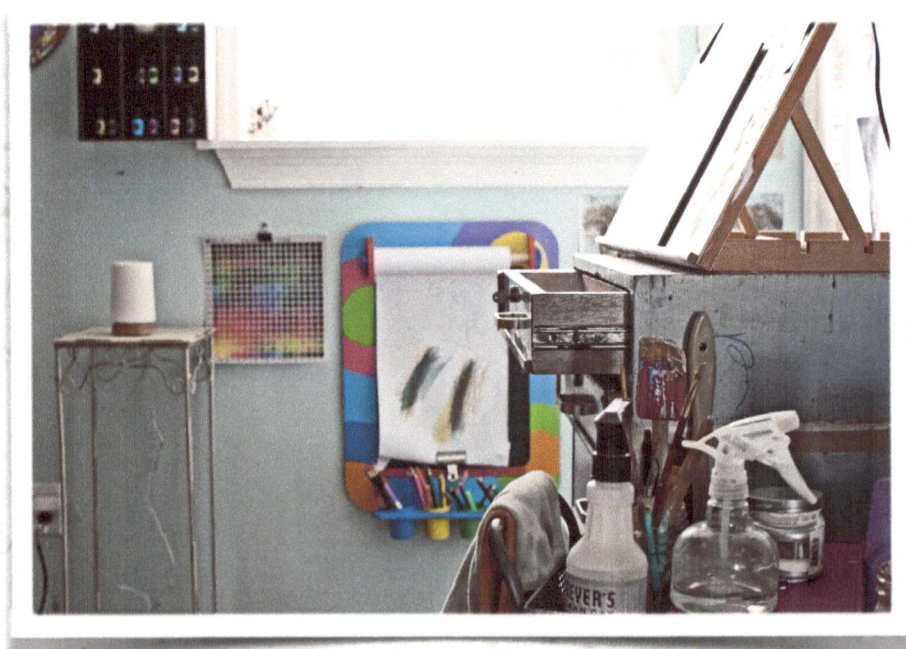

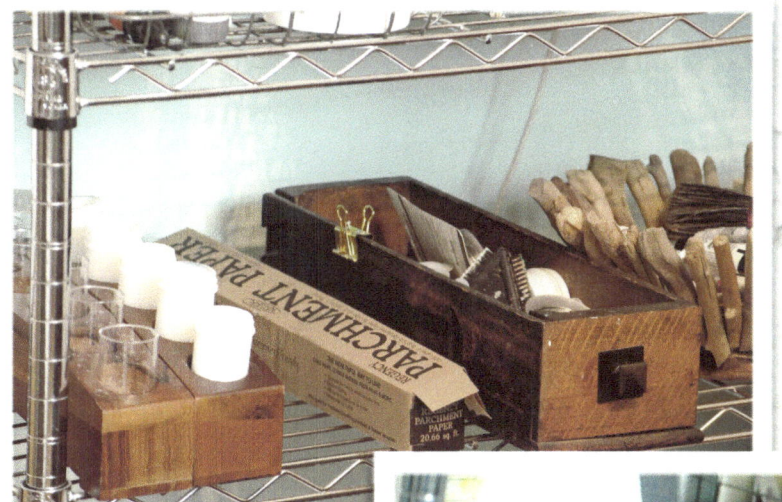

I'm pretty sure
I have an
inordinate affection
for art supplies.

But I have to have
the kind of art supply
that IS art,
all by itself.

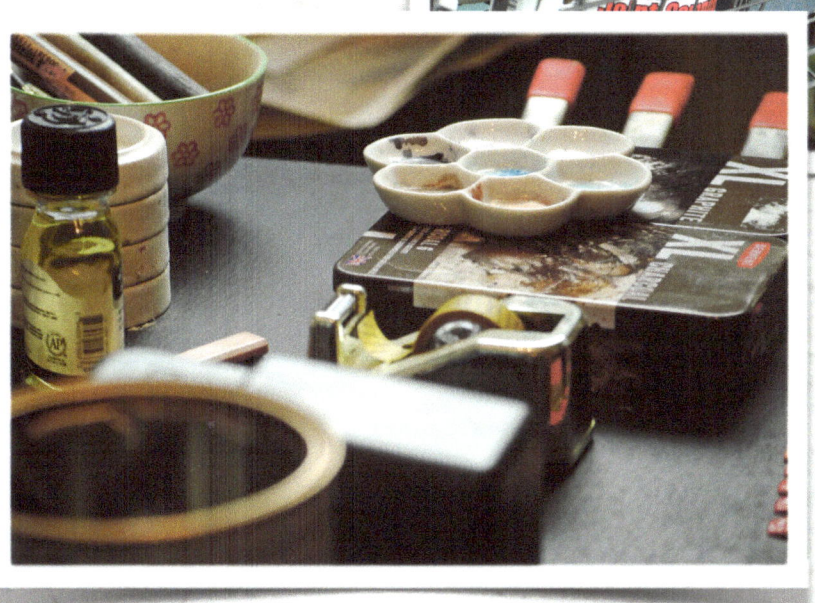

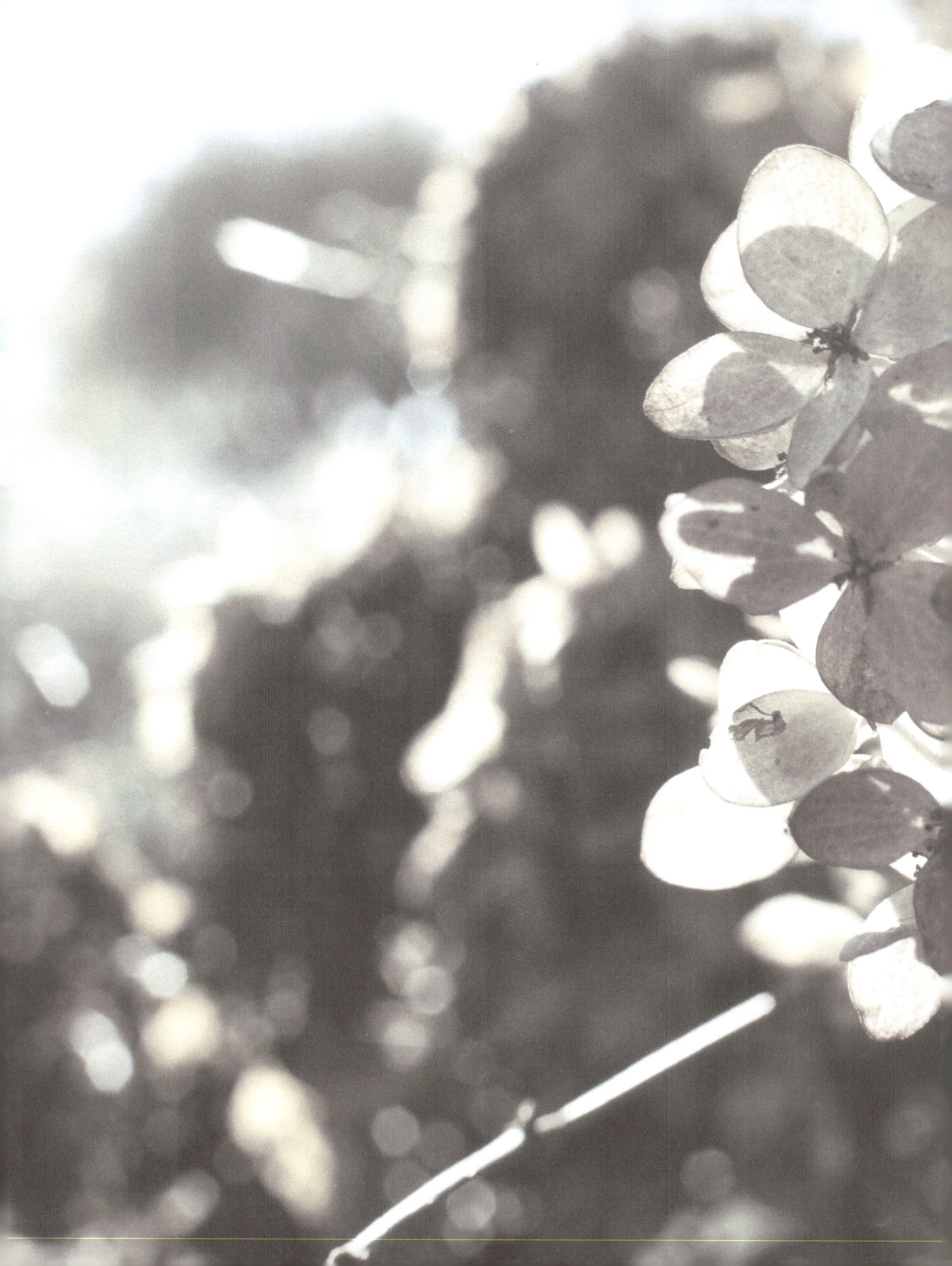

Rehab

("the harlot")

How is your Advent season coming along?

I hope this book becomes one place
where you can gather yourself.

I hope these pages help you
take your scattered bits of time,
scattered attention,
scattered devotion,
scattered energies...

...and offer them to a gathering God
who can take our scattered remains
and create twelve baskets of blessing.

My mother once told a funny story about how, when she was a child, she used to belt out "Jesus Loves Me" at the top of her lungs...only she always sang it this way, "...little ones do limp along, they are weak, but He is strong!"

This reminded me of a little guy I used to keep in the church nursery, years ago. He asked this question: "Why does Jesus call us kids 'weak butts'?" If you put all that together, you get, "Little ones do limp along, they are weak butts, He is strong."

As a little girl, I used to sing "Silent Night", and wonder why the mother and holy infant, so tender and mild, slept in heavenly PEAS.

It is frighteningly easy to mishear important information. Jesus in Luke 8 said "Be careful how you hear." Then, in Luke 10, in a different context, Jesus said, "Be careful how you read, or 'How readest thou?' God's word is anything but merely information. It is alive and active, when we believe.

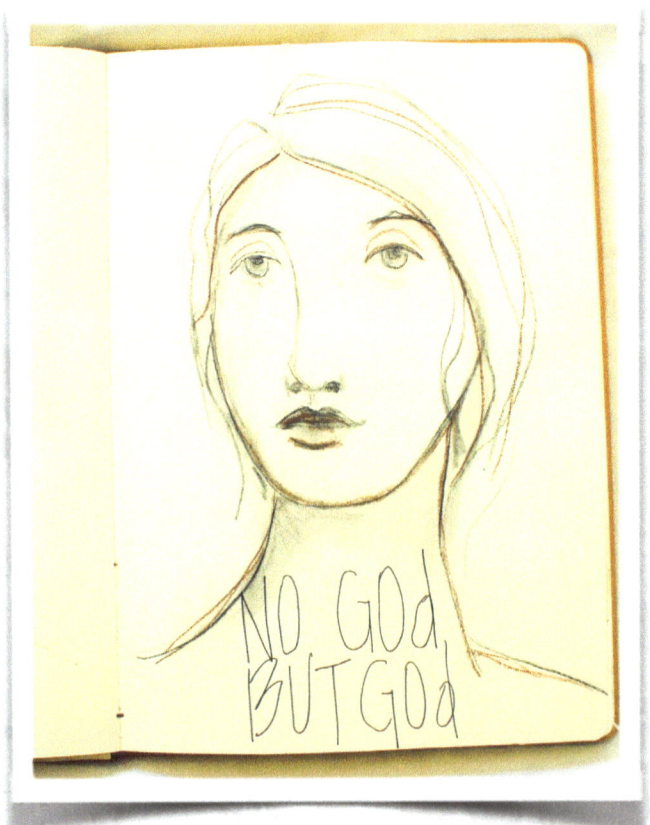

Rehab - the harlot who possessed
the wisdom and
the revelation of a great apostle:

"For I know...
...that your God IS God
in heaven above
and on earth below."

There is information, but that information is meant to INWARDLY FORM us...to fundamentally change our perspective. God will not be "telling us something", He will be revealing Himself. The Bible is a narrative, not a text book. We are invited to participate in the ongoing narrative, but we don't control it. Our modern preference is for information over story. We would rather gather principles and information that we can quantify and bullet point and apply. But God comes to us in story for the most part. We can't live up to what is revealed, but we can live into what is revealed.

Of the Women of Advent, our second woman's name was Rahab. Her middle name was "the" and her last name was "harlot". No kidding! In all of scripture, she is referred to, in both old and new testaments, as Rahab the Harlot. Sort of like "Winnie the Pooh".

Just a thought: How would you like to be forever identified by your besetting sin? "There's Brenda the gossip. John the addict. Hazel the fornicator. There goes Bill the liar."

This is a page from one of my many sketchbooks. She was rendered in charcoal, Stabilo pencil, Inktense pencil, and white gesso, with oil pastel crayon for tiny, colorful, gestural accents.

I love how she turned out. Something about the eyes...

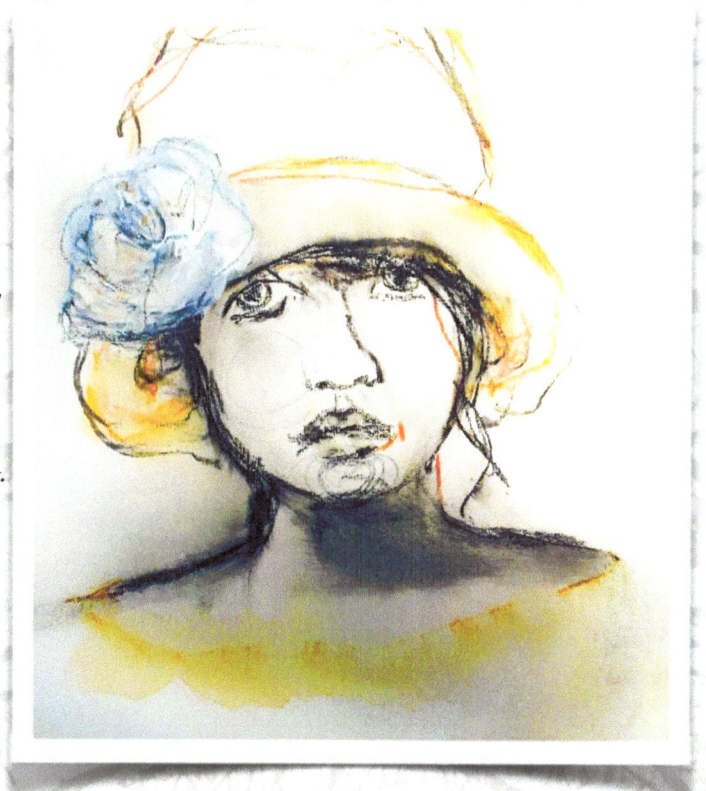

Let's set up our back story. Moses had died. Now, we cannot identify with all of Israel's profound sense of national lostness, the feeling of disconnect those Israelites felt. As Americans, we change leaders every 4-8 years. Moses was the leader of a lifetime. They had known no other leader. He was their link to God, their intercessor, their law giver.

After a respectable period of mourning, God matter-of-factly says to the people "Moses my servant is dead. Joshua is your new leader. Let the past go, cheer up ("be of good courage") and move on." Today, we'd think that constitutes a lack of good people skills. But hearts have to be called up higher, or promise dies.

Can I say that again? "Hearts have to be called up higher, or promise dies."

The Promised Land still was yet just that...just a promise. God's people were going to have to fight for it. In fact, there would be a multitude of battles waged, as God's people took ground, sometimes literally yard by yard. Only one of many such battles was the battle of Jericho.

Rahab's Jericho was an Amorite civilization - a pagan culture, given to passing people through fire, and of child sacrifice too horrific to speak of. The physical city itself was built as a monument to insurmountability. There were TWO walls in this city, an inner wall and an outer wall. Between these two walls there was a 12-15' gap, and across this gap there were timbers laid, forming the foundation for sun baked brick houses. One of these houses belong to Rahab.

The.

Harlot.

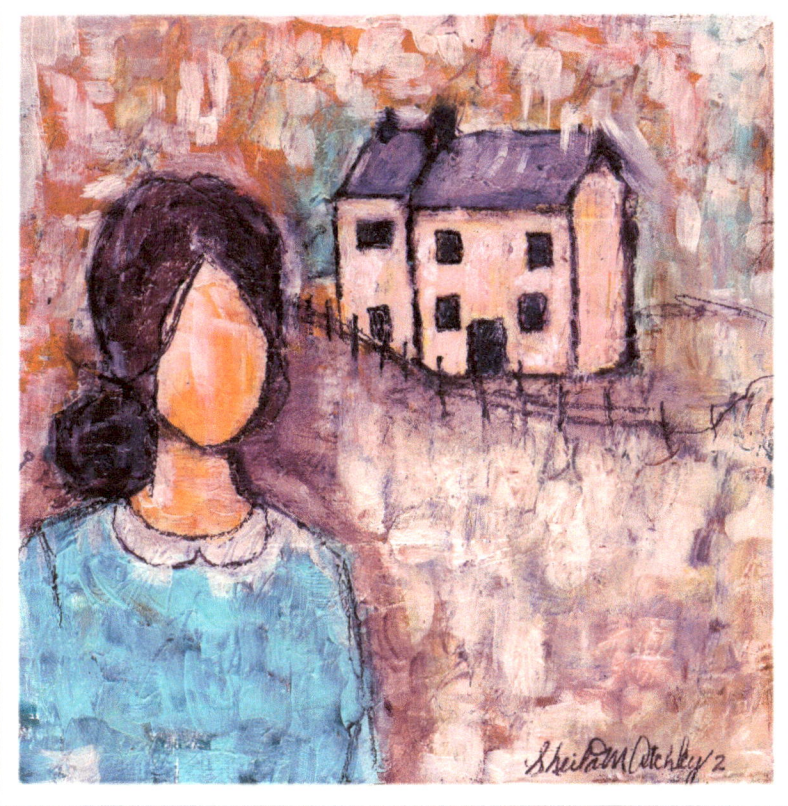

HOME
is a recurring theme in
my art.

I often wonder what Rahab
(the. harlot)'s home looked
like.

I wonder what her
decorating style was? We
know it likely
involved the color red.

I can't stop
rendering faces. I think
that, of all God made -
mountains and flowers and
animals -
people are His favorite,
too.

The human face captivates.

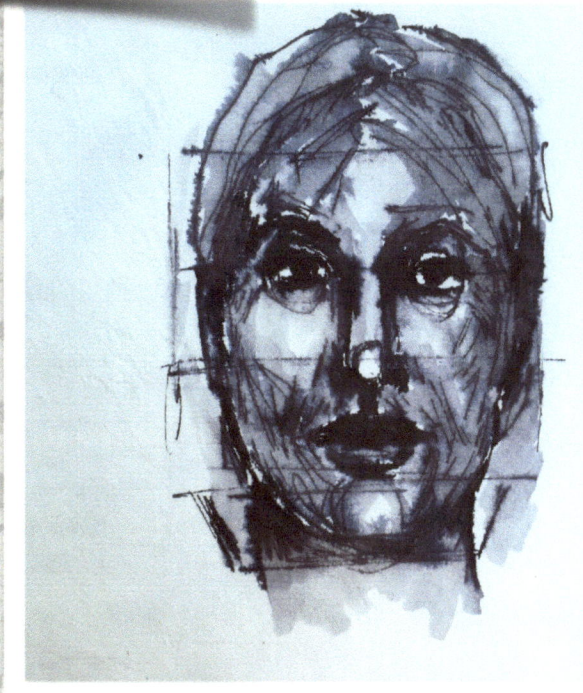

Joshua, having freshly taken command, sends two spies into the city. They infiltrated the city - I imagine Tom Cruise, Mission Impossible style, only without the technology. This was very high drama. They wound up at Rahab's house. (cough) In their defense, in that culture, brothels were also sort of bed and breakfasts...a place to stay overnight.

But soon there is an urgent problem. The king has spies throughout the city, and he has sent guards to Rahab's house, banging on the door.

Rahab hides the two men on her roof. And she tells a huge lie to the guards, "Oopsie! Those men were spies? I had no idea! I didn't didn't know ! They went that way! If you hurry you will catch them!"

So she sends the soldiers on a wild goose chase, and goes to the roof and initiates a conversation with the 2 Israeli spies. Her words are passionate and intelligent. Let's pick it up right there in Joshua 2:8

8 Before the spies lay down for the night, she went up on the roof 9 and said to them, "I know that the Lord has given you this land and that a great fear of you has fallen on us, so that all who live in this country are melting in fear because of you. 10 We have heard how the Lord dried up the water of the Red Sea[a] for you when you came out of Egypt, and what you did to Sihon and Og, the two kings of the Amorites east of the Jordan, whom you completely destroyed.[b] 11 When we heard of it, our hearts melted in fear and everyone's courage failed because of you, for the Lord your God is God in heaven above and on the earth below.

12 "Now then, please swear to me by the Lord that you will show kindness to my family, because I have shown kindness to you. Give me a sure sign 13 that you will spare the lives of my father and mother, my brothers and sisters, and all who belong to them—and that you will save us from death."

Her words here remind me of II Tim 1:12 when Paul, the great apostle, says, "I know in Whom I have believed..." or of righteous Job when he said, "I know my redeemer lives!" But these are the words of a prostitute. Never, ever judge a book by its cover.

Rehab was a woman of faith. She believed for what she
could not, to receive what she should not. She was
ignited into action.

In Tamar's story, we saw that injustice is no barrier to
birthing big things. In Rahab's story, we see that a
woman's past is no barrier to birthing big things.

Rahab experienced a type and shadow of salvation. Rahab
had this scarlet cord, see. I think it was braided flax,
and must have been very long and strong enough to hold at
least two men. This scarlet cord becomes her salvation.
She sends the spies away by letting them down the wall
with this cord, with the plan that she would leave it
exactly as it hung, there in the window, as a signal to
the Israelite army to save that one house alive, and all
that was in it.

You must realize that this had to have presented a whole
new set of problems. After all, she had just told at
least 2 soldiers - guards - that she saw 2 Israelites go
out by the gate. Twenty minutes AFTER she tells them
this, there is a red rope hanging out her back window and
down the wall? Think about it. She could be in some
serious trouble.

My friend, taking big risks is part of the adventure.
Take some chances!

The spies stole away. Rahab didn't know exactly how her
family would be spared, only God knew the plan at that
moment. But I imagine she felt pretty good about being up
on that massive wall. Yet she was in the most dangerous
spot in the known world - like finding yourself on the
deck of the Titanic. Her home stood directly on top of a
wall that would soon crumble into dust.

The true safety of that entire house stood on the promises
of God, and on the faith of the one woman in it.

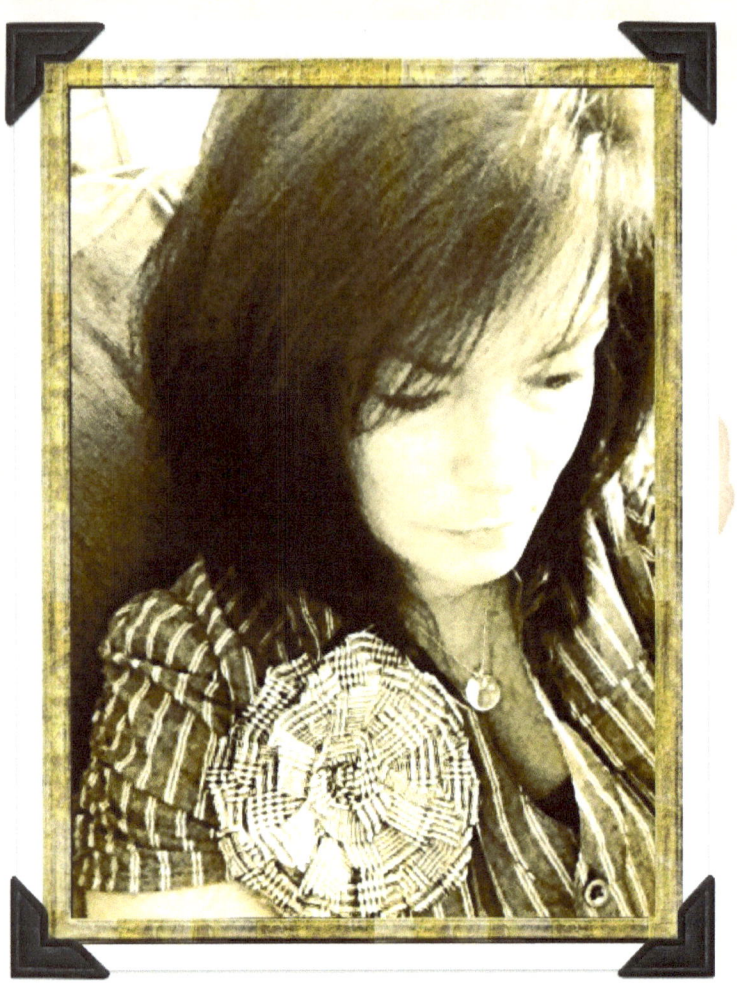

Women of all ages
and all seasons
need to have aspirations.

My 70-plus-year-old
mother is such an inspiration
to me.

She is just now re-discovering
her love for art!
She is making me see
where my creativity came from.

You are never too old.
You are never too young.

Take initiative!

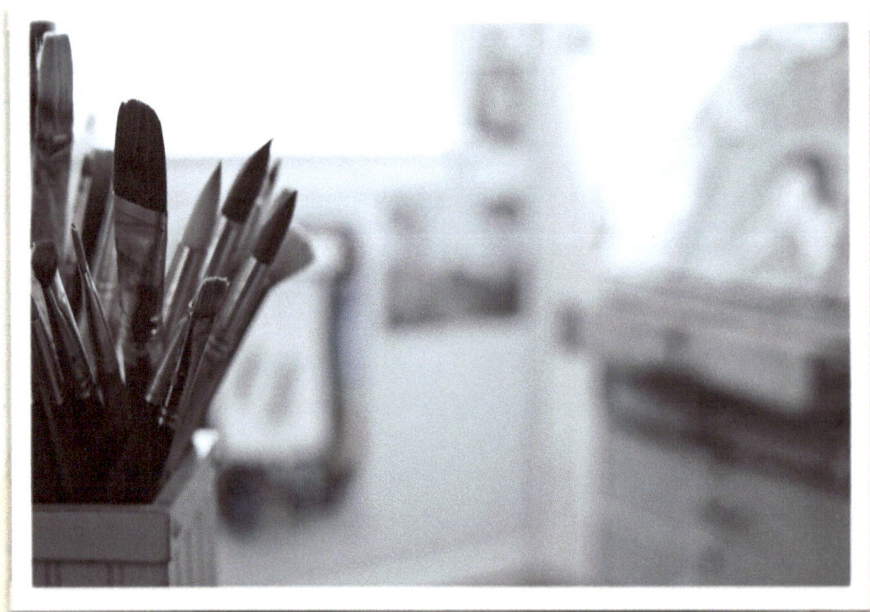

I did not discover my passion for art until my (quite) late 40's!
As I pursued this strange, new passion full=on, taking massive initiative,
I began to have a bit of an inner conflict.
I felt torn, because I have always, always been a "message" girl.
I am all about the message of grace. I am all about words. However, I found myself becoming as drawn to
image, as I had always been to words. I was finding myself fully, passionately,
and equally drawn to writing and to art. What to do? I only have so many hours in a day!
Well.   We are always so much better together than we are alone.
My daughter is the one who suggested I write this book, and combine it with my art.
This was a light-bulb moment. Perfection! For the first time,
the two have come together. . .my life makes sense. . .
. . .and I couldn't be more pleased.

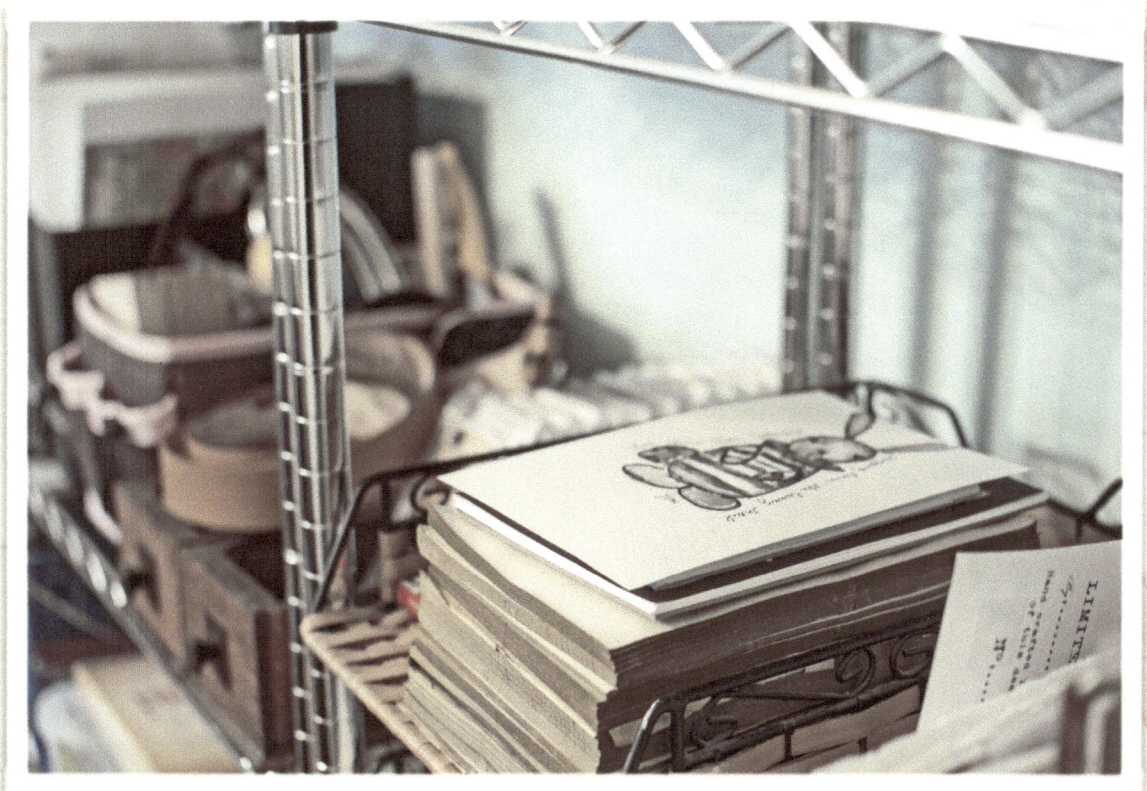

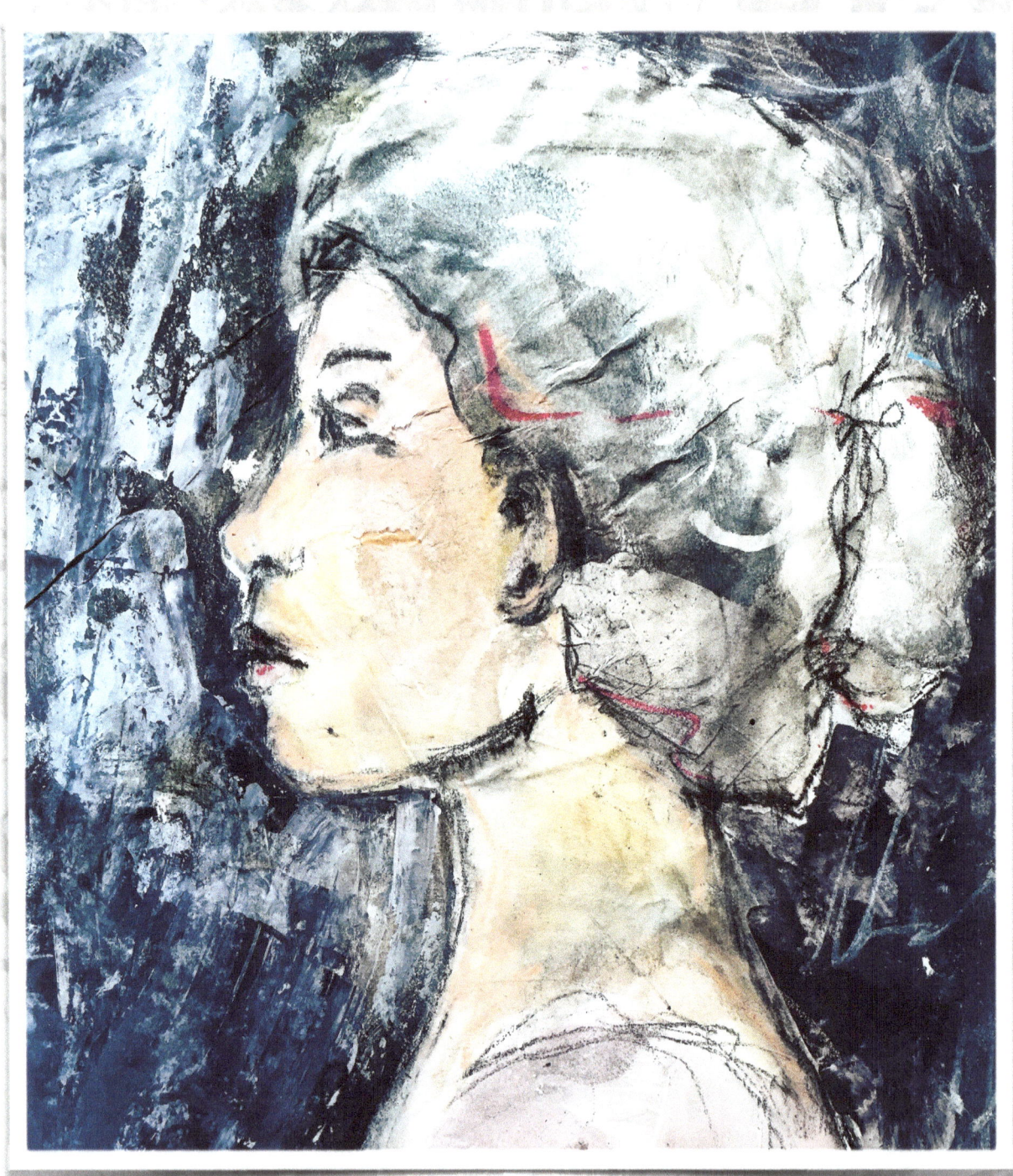

This is the way I imagine Rahab. Strong and regal.
I love the scarlet thread of oil pastel that appears in her hair...

Time went by. Still she waited. Day followed day. She
watched the hot desert horizon and waited. It was the
waiting that was excruciating.

One day, far in the distance, she finally saw a cloud of
dust - a massive army of Israelites approaching the city!
Instantly, Jericho became a noisy, terrified hub of frantic
activity. Soldiers manning their stations, everyone
preparing for the worst. Rahab couldn't leave the window,
as she watched in nervous fascination the famous army of
Israel getting closer and closer. But instead of shields
and spears, she saw men in curious robes, with poles on
their shoulders, carrying an odd box with curtains on it.
A few others were carrying these long, curved horns. She
waited for the bloodshed to begin, only to see the whole
lot of them hang a left and begin circling the city. They
marched around once, in complete silence, blew their
horns...

...and left.

How. Very. Odd.

Then it happened again the second day. And the third. And
the fourth. Every day, complete silence that got more and
more eerie. Every day, the single, long blast of the
horns. By this time, the whole city was unhinged.

Then the 7th day came. Again, the cloud of dust, again the
massive army approaches the city. Again, they turn left
and begin to circle. Only this time they went
around. . .and around. . .and around. . .they started early
in the morning, and it went on all day. As you know, after
the 7th time around, the trumpets sounded, only this time
the blast was accompanied by a terrifying sound - every
Israelite man, shouting.

NOT the typical battle cry...this cry sounded like...this
cry in fact was a ...VICTORY SHOUT! A celebration! Every
man shouted as though the battle had been already won.

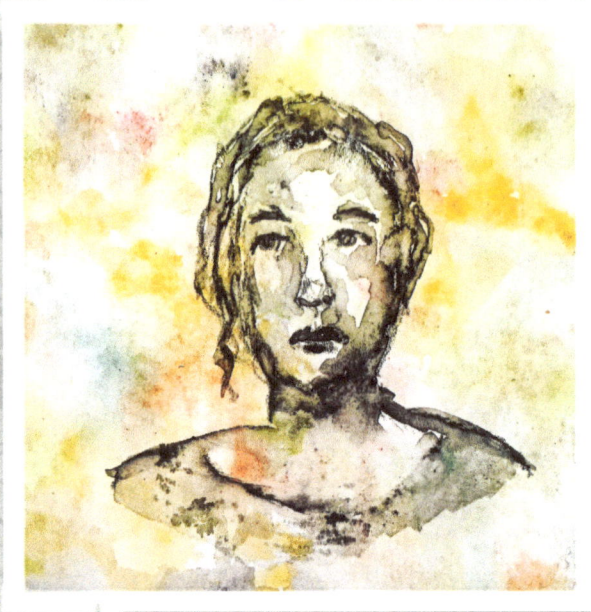

Another, more colorful
perspective of Rahab.

I created a watercolor background, then
sealed it with matte medium.
Lastly, I sketched Rahab with water
soluble pencil, going over my marks with water.

Below, an original poem . . .

Oh soul, tightly shut up,

Fly thee to the home of the harlot,

To that acknowledged place of chains and

Servitude to sin;

That place where your skin is

Your only hiding place;

Where mercy, like scarlet, awaits;

That place where what has been, even today,

Is no obstacle to scandalous grace.

Fly there, soul, when all that you have

Ever trusted in collapses left and right.

Leave not this house of no pretense

Till all else is dust, and the Red Rope

Lowers you down that one last wall,

And you walk away, restored.

By Sheila Atchley

Then there was the rumbling, the thunder, it all was a terrifying blur in Rahab's memory, I am sure, as those massive walls - those monuments to insurmountability, in a moment became a pile of rubble and choking, blinding dust. I mean no disrespect, but I want you to consider the images most of you have in your minds of 9/11 when the two towers fell. That kind of dust.

A prostitute saved. Her whole household saved. Saved by the same promises and same scarlet cord that runs from Genesis to Revelation.

If you then read the "begets", you discover that a prostitute becomes the great-great grandmother to the next king of Israel. Rahab the harlot. Her business was to profane that which was sacred. God not only delivered her from death, but gave her back the most precious and squandered thing in her life...true intimacy. God gave Rahab a romance. Rahab marries Salmon, and many scholars believe he was one of those 2 spies. This is epic romance! "Boy meets girl, girl meets boy, girl hides boy, boy rescues girl..."

Rahab is remembered in Hebrews 11 as a woman of faith - one of only 2 mentioned in that passage, and God placed her in the lineage of King David, but not only of King David, but of God Himself. He chose this prostitute to take a place of honor in His ancestry.

Remember the words of Mary, when she was given a glimpse of God's plan for her?

"How can these things happen, seeing as I have never known a man?"

Had Rahab been given a glimpse of what she would be birthing into the earth, she would have wept and exclaimed, "How can these things be, seeing as I have known many, many men?"

Your past is of no consequence to God. Oh, become alive with possibility for your destiny, no matter what your history may be!

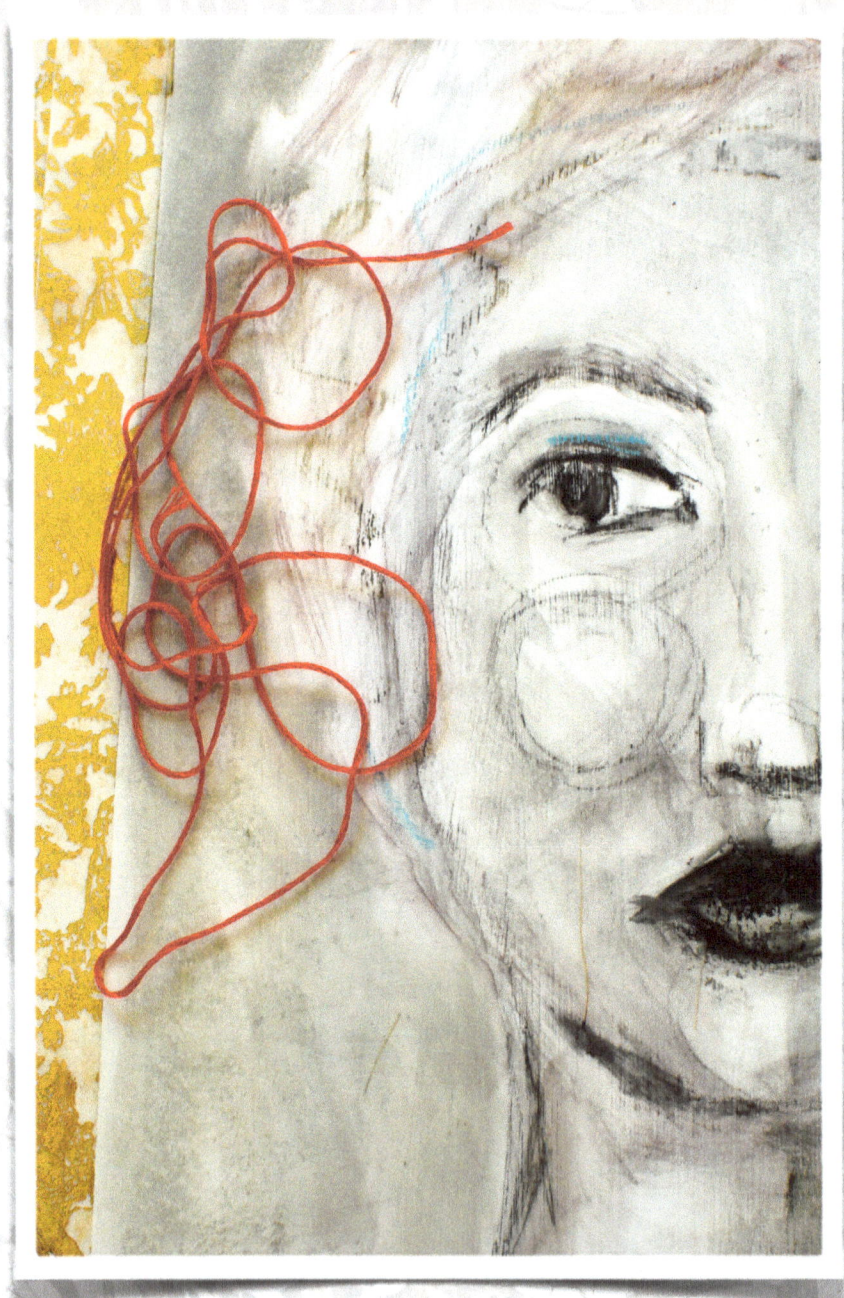

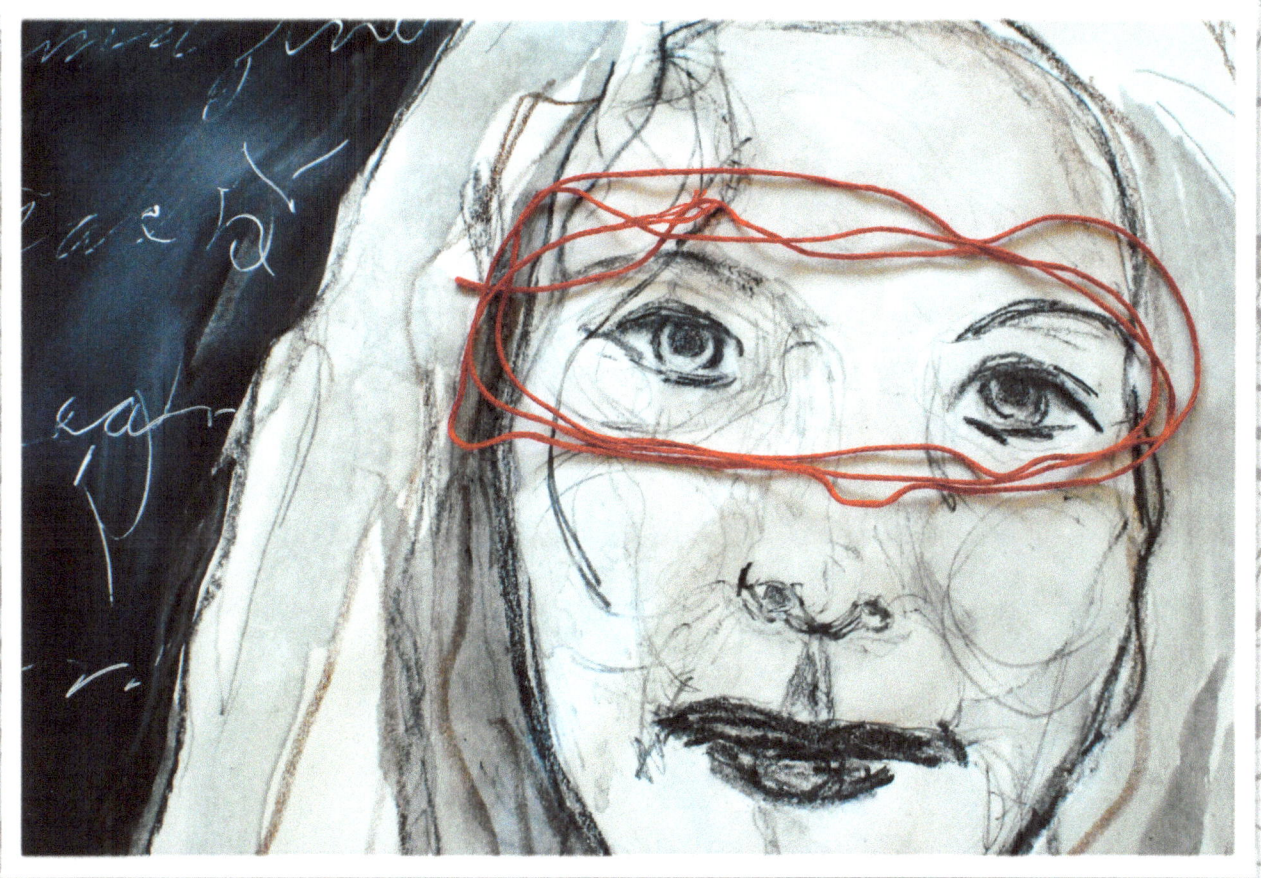

This is a self portrait,
rendered in graphite pencil, three colors of Stabilo pencil, and watercolor, on heavy paper.
Next, I used black gesso,
and painted around my head, treating it as negative space, (as opposed to painting the background first,
and gesso'ing a face or form over that). Then, I scripted words in white ink, and added the scarlet thread,
just before photographing the page.

The scarlet cord is my salvation, too, and it is the lens through which I view all of life.

journaling questions

"Asking questions is of inestimable importance"

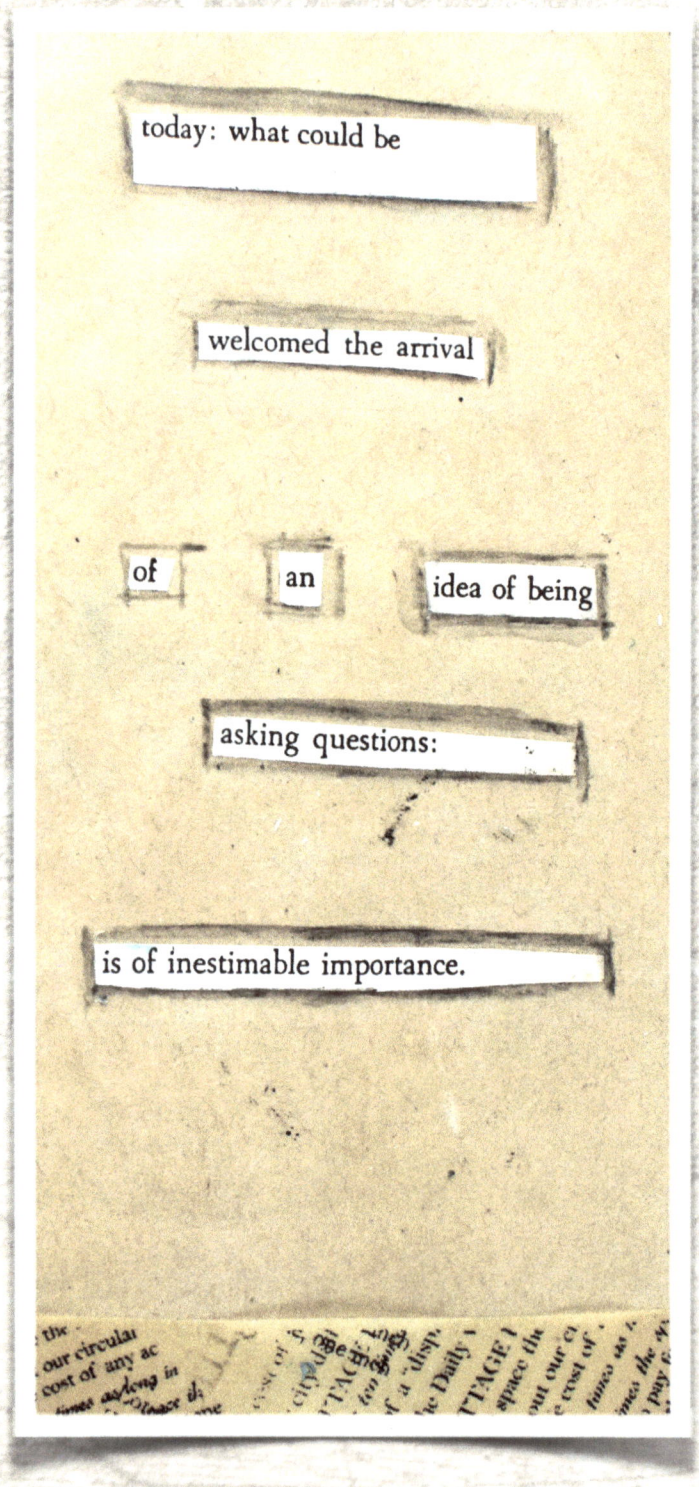

Based on the lives of Tamar and Rahab,
compare your present situation with what is possible:

_____
_____
_____
_____
_____
_____
_____

God is always up to a "new thing". The arrival of the
next new thing is always pending. What is it you need to
welcome into your life? (Do not write about what needs to
go…write about what you want to see ushered in!)

_____
_____
_____
_____
_____
_____
_____

Your initiative is a way of seeing. It is a fresh idea of
being in the world. Choose one thing you want to do
differently, and write about it:

_____
_____
_____
_____
_____
_____
_____

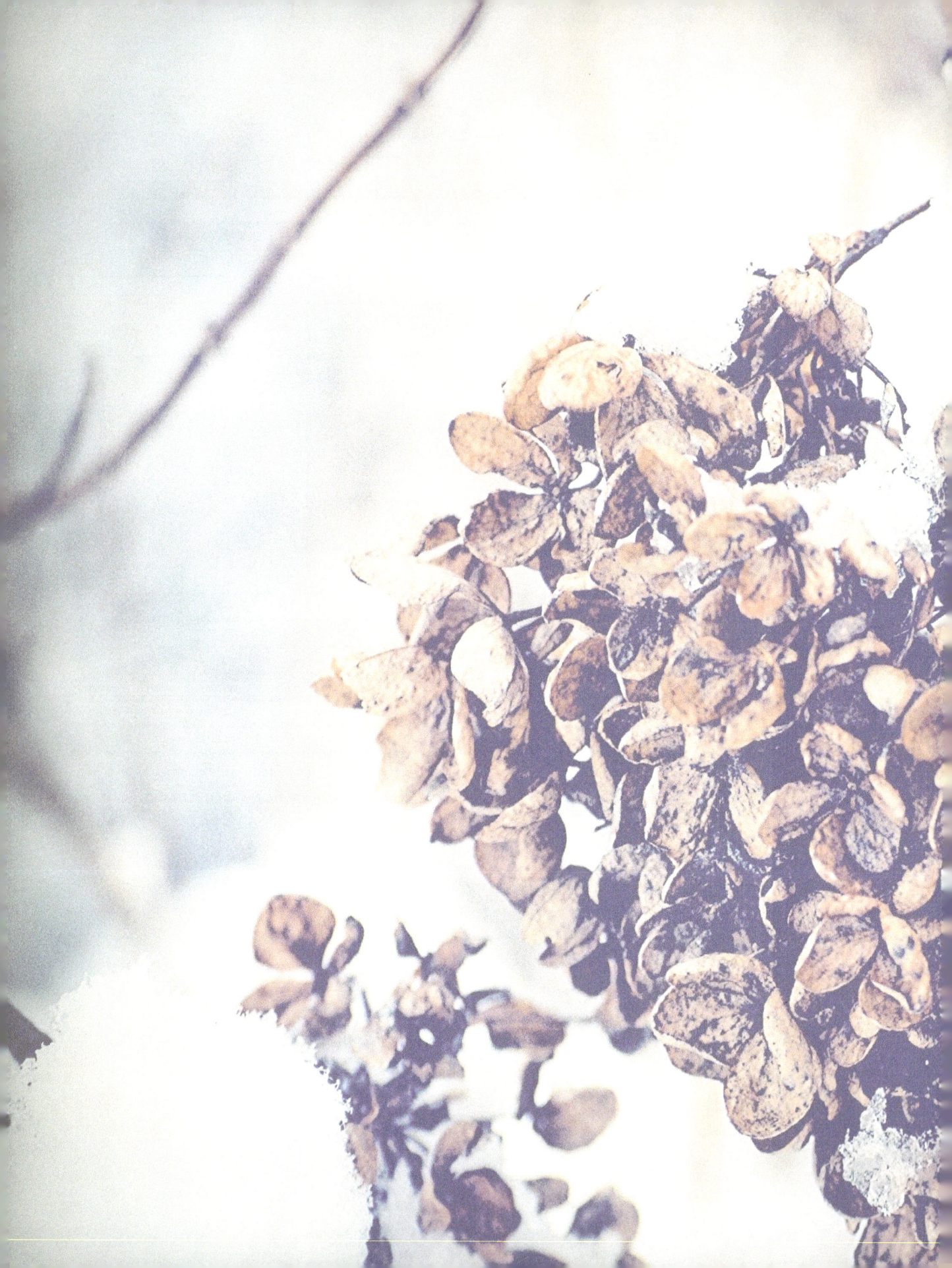

week two

Ruth

KINSHIP AND A
KINSMAN REDEEMER

and

Bathsheba

"I AM PREGNANT"

Come with me on an exploration
of friendship.

First, we find Ruth, who knew what it meant
to have the love and counsel of another woman.
She reaped the benefits of
being seen and heard.

And then, we find Bathsheba,
who didn't seem to have
a friend in the world...

Lastly, we will touch on
the remarkable friendship
between God's sovereignty and our free will.

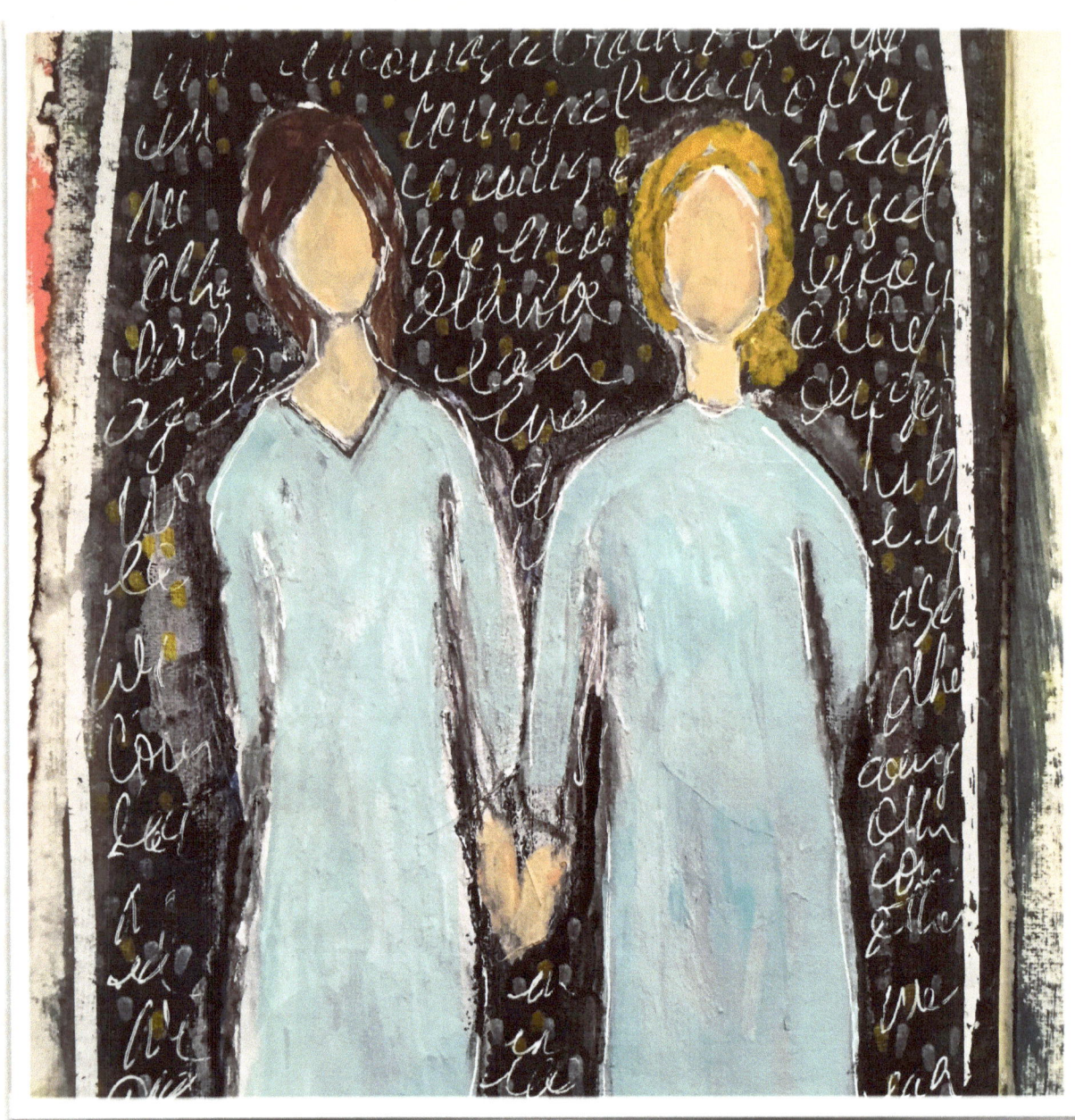

Who hasn't longed for a kinship
like that of Ruth and Naomi?

"Now it came to pass in the days when the judges ruled, that there was a famine in the land."

In the theater of my imagination, I hear the thrumming bass voice of a narrator, and his tone is ominous as he reads the above words. . .I see the page of a well-worn Bible turning, as if being blown by a breeze - as we begin the story of Ruth.

Here is what we need to understand about this true and story-book beginning of the Biblical account of Ruth: Far from a Dickens-ian novel, with its iconic opener, "It was the best of times, it was the worst of times", the book of Ruth begins very darkly. Nothing but darkly. "It was the worst of times, it was the worst of the worst of times." The time of the judges, particularly in the setting of this story, was an oppressive time when "every man did what was right in his own eyes."

This story begins with anarchy, corrupt government, famine, grief, and death. We are introduced to Naomi and her two daughters-in-law Orpah and Ruth. We read in verse 7 of Ruth chapter 1:

"Wherefore Naomi went forth out of the place where she was. . .to return to the land of Judah."

And so the account of God's deliverance begins then, as it still begins today: with us leaving the place where we once were, with us finally becoming tired of feeling stuck and starving. Again we find God's sovereignty married to a woman's initiative.

Naomi had been living in Moab, where tragedy strikes, as all three men - Naomi's husband and her two sons - die untimely deaths. Naomi decides to return to her homeland, but Ruth, who had been born a Moabite, chooses to immigrate.

At this point in history, as in Tamar's day, widows had no property rights, no value, and no protection or provision. The mistreatment of widows was common practice – but if you were an immigrant and a widow, you were guaranteed to be abused.

Naomi pours out her bitterness of heart, and instructs her daughters-in-law to return to Moab, where they have a chance of remarrying. Orpah decides to return, but the Scriptures say "Ruth clave to Naomi."

The German poet Goethe called the book of Ruth "the most beautiful short story in the world, the loveliest short story that has ever been written". In part, I believe, Goethe was smitten with the following passage, one which, though it is often recited at weddings, is in fact the most moving words regarding the friendship of women ever written:

"Intreat me not to leave you, or to return from following you: for where you go, I will go, and where you lodge, I will lodge. Your people shall be my people, and your God, my God. Where you die, I will die, and there will I be buried: the Lord do so to me, and more also, if anything but death parts you and I."

Ruth's response to Naomi's plea is to commit herself to Naomi, and to immigrate to Naomi's land, to be part of Naomi's Jewish race, and of Naomi's faith. Ruth commits her entire life. A conversion takes place here; Ruth has become a believer. Her choice is made with no certainty that she will be welcome or even safe in Bethlehem, where she is going.

Is conversion any different today, really? Does being in Christ give us a cosmic guarantee that we will be loved and safe and happy, with personal peace and affluence? Or is the guarantee more that of "in this world you will have trouble, but be of good cheer. . ." . These are worthy questions.

This extraordinary conversion is the point of dramatic shift in the story. This is the turning point, where all of history pivots towards a redemption song. God intervenes to bless Ruth and Naomi, in small acts of divine providence that add up to uncommon ordinary miracles.

They came home to Bethlehem, arriving in the beginning of barley harvest. A few days after this homecoming, we find Ruth gleaning barley in a field, to feed herself and her mother-in-law. I love how scripture puts it, in the King James version. It says in verse 3 of Ruth chapter 2, "*and her hap was to light on a part of the field belonging to Boaz...*"

If Ruth were with us today, sitting in leather chairs around a knee-high table at Starbucks, she would brood for a moment, sipping her venti caramel. Then, she'd fasten her dark eyes on you, and with a toss of her wavy brunette hair, she'd declare with conviction, straight into you:

"When you take initiative and obey the Lord to leave your stuck and starving, faithless space, God will see to it that your hap is to light in the right place at the right appointed time."

It "just so happened" that she ended up in Boaz' field. I know you are just so glad that it just so happened that way! If it hadn't "just so happened", then we can forget about certain shepherds who just so happened to be in perhaps the same field in the same Bethlehem, 1100 years later, "keeping watch over their flocks by night, and lo, and angel of the Lord came upon them and the glory of God shone all around them. . ."

Ruth didn't know it that day, but the Christ child would be a direct descendant of Ruth and Boaz.

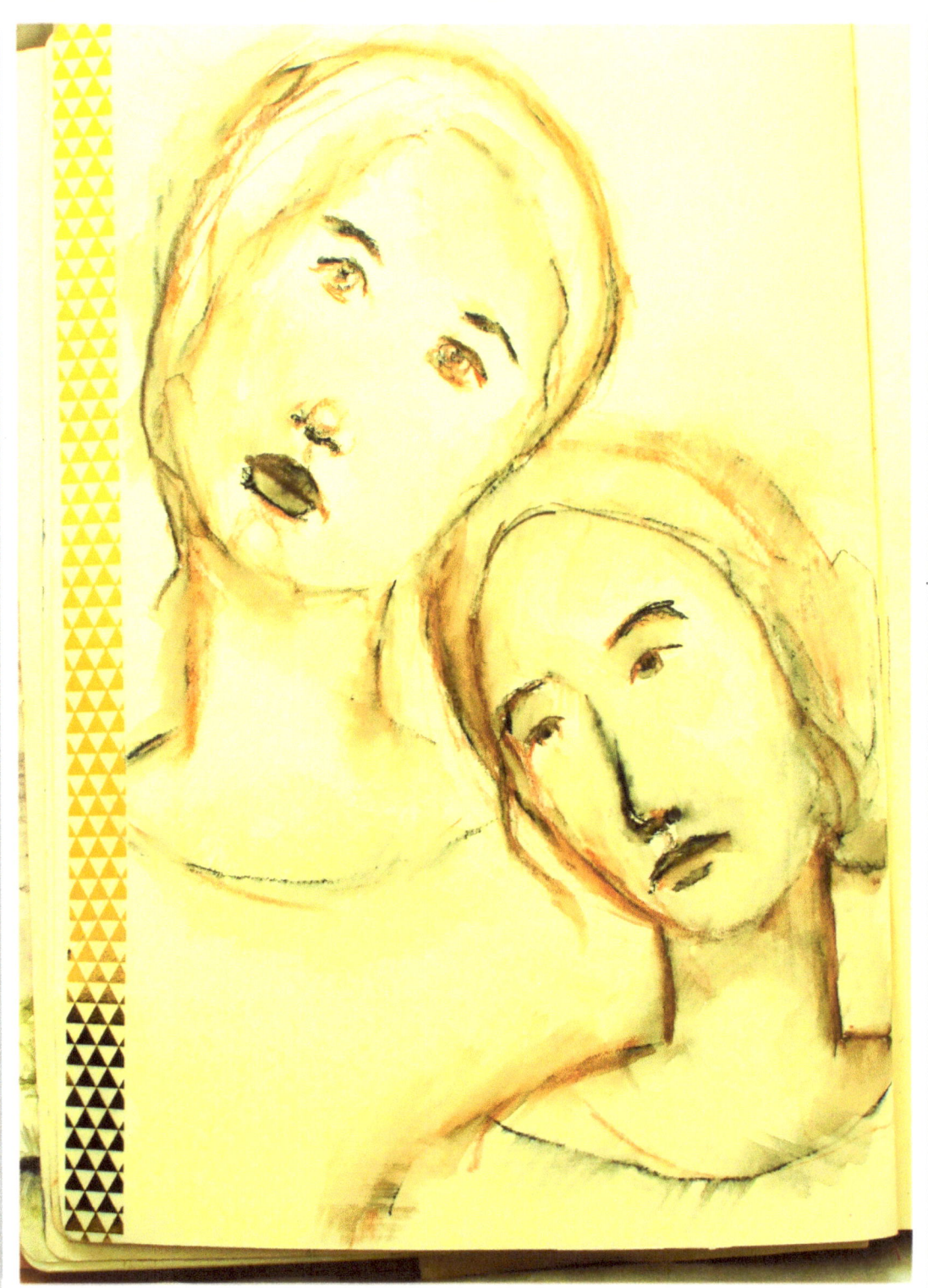

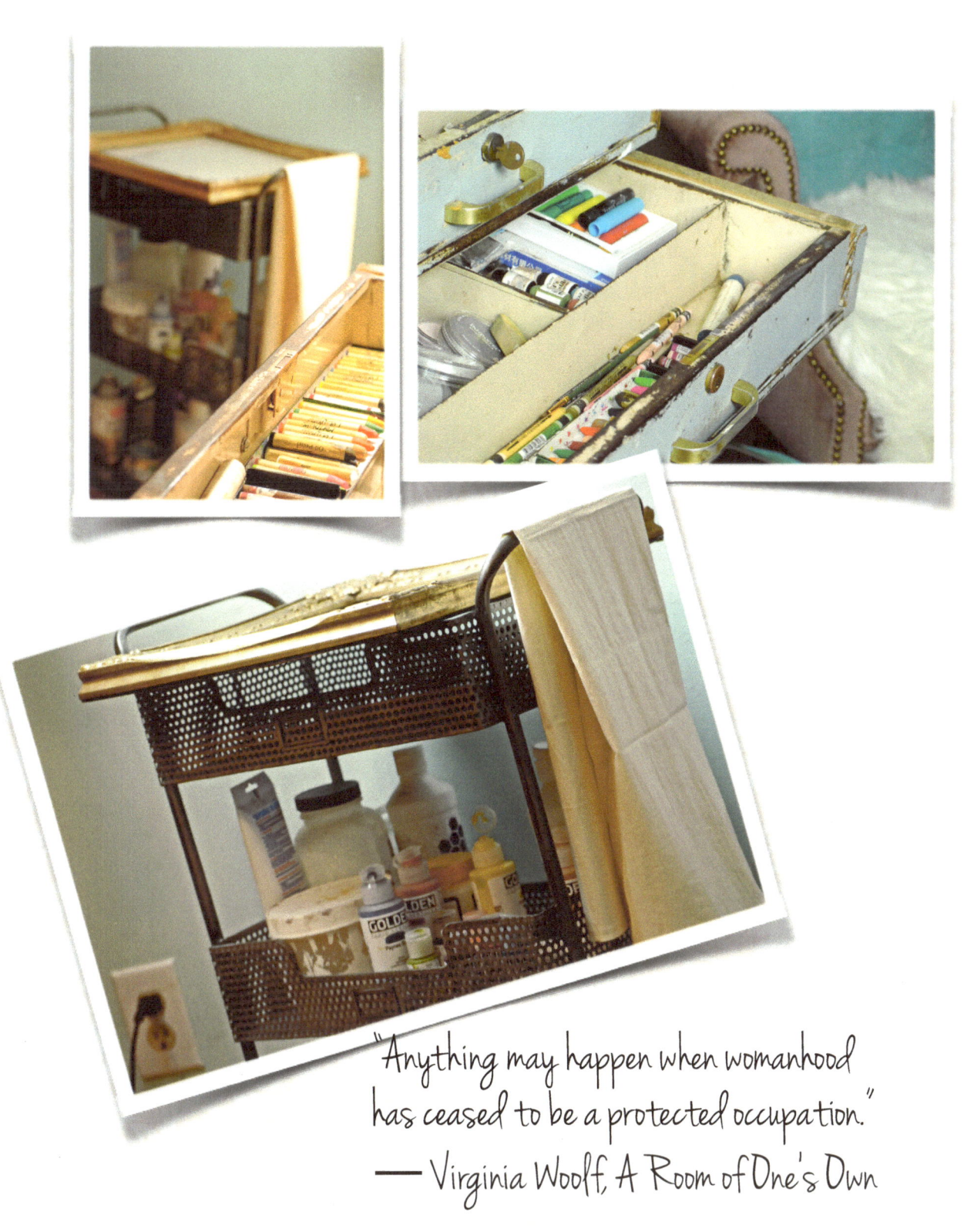

"Anything may happen when womanhood has ceased to be a protected occupation."
— Virginia Woolf, *A Room of One's Own*

The happy truth that we can glean, right alongside Ruth and her barley, is that Ruth most certainly got up that morning not knowing where she would end up. She got dressed, not knowing that she would become an ancestor to God. She was simply committed to Him, and so quietly, without any indication, God was working for her good and His glory. Widowed Ruth did what she could do, which was to wake up, get up, dress up, and show up, every single day, regardless of her pain and grief and emotional state. God did the rest.

As I sit here, sipping my own version of a venti-caramel, reading those last two sentences, tears sting my eyes. Because, though I am not widowed (thank God), I have the same story. I've battled long nights of friends' betrayal, prodigal sons, back pain, restless legs, and clinical depression. Those many nights were inexorably followed by many mornings where only obedience to the call of God got me out of my bed. I woke up, got up, dressed up, and showed up every day, regardless of my emotions, and God did the rest. This book you hold in your hands is tangible proof that He is able.

Since widows had no means of livelihood, Ruth gleans barley behind the harvesters in a field where she can only hope the owner will treat her favorably. The chances of that are slim, because Ruth was: 1. impoverished, 2. a widow 3. a woman, and 4. an immigrant - a Moabitess. For her to show up, hoping to work safely, was an act of great faith on her part. Her well-being was dependent on the owner of the field being willing to keep certain laws that most men, in fact, did not keep - laws that God had set in place, laws meant to give widows and orphans a measure of provision and protection.

Ah, but her "hap was to light" in the field of a good, good man. Ruth landed in the field of a man who, we see in verse 9 of chapter 2, had charged every young man in the area not to so much as lay a finger on her. Ruth landed in the field of a man who also made sure that extra barley was purposefully left behind for her, because he had heard of her amazing immigration story, and of her sacrificial love for her Jewish mother-in-law.

Later in the narrative, Ruth does discover that Boaz is a near-relative, who has the power to buy back all that has been lost to Naomi and to her. The only catch is that Ruth has to be part of the deal. It isn't merely an issue of Boaz having legal right to buy back the land forfeited by Naomi's late husband, he would also have to marry Ruth and raise children with her.

In an unbearably romantic move, Ruth again takes extreme initiative, and dresses in what historians say was wedding garments. She showed up at the bed of Boaz, late at night, and laid at his feet until he woke up. I love how scripture says, "She came softly. . ."

Boaz awoke with a start and demanded to know who was laying at his feet. Ruth tremblingly discloses her identity, and promptly proposes marriage:

"I am Ruth thy handmaid: spread therefore thy skirt over thy handmaid; for thou art a near kinsman!"

Please do not picture this the way it may have been told to you in Sunday school. This was a passionate exchange. This was dreamy. Boaz knew who Ruth was, now, and he knew he thought she was amazing in all kinds of ways. Boaz intimates that he feels that her proposal is almost too good to be true. He assures her that he will do all in his power to become her kinsman redeemer. . .her man.

Except for one, little thing.

". . .howbeit, there is a kinsman nearer than I."

There was another man Boaz was aware of, who was actually a little closer to Naomi, in the bloodline. This man, by law, had to be offered first dibs on the property of Naomi's dead husband, Elimilech. Boaz promises to see to the matter immediately, as soon as the sun came up.

Then, in an unbearably romantic gesture of his own, he asks her to lay at his feet until morning. He didn't touch Ruth, but he was beautifully aware of her presence at his feet, so near to his touch, yet so far away from any right to touch her, yet. all. night. long. I doubt either of them slept much, but Boaz very much wanted to keep the woman he loved safe from traveling back to her home at night.

Just before the sun came up, he sent her home, but not without filling her veil with grain so that it looked like she had a good reason to be out and about.

True to his word, Boaz went straight to the gate of the city, and identified the man who was the closer relation. He plays his cards carefully and brilliantly, and with the element of surprise. He casually calls the name of the man, getting his attention, and then quickly letting the "nearer kinsman" know that a parcel of land once belonging to Elimilech had come available.

"And I thought to tell you about it, thinking you may want to buy it. I just so happen to have ten elders here to witness the purchase, if you want it. If you don't want it, tell me now, because I think I might buy it."

The man answered "Sure. I will redeem it."

Then Boaz chimed in, "There's just one thing. There's this girl - an immigrant girl by the name of Ruth. She is part of the deal, and you sort of by law also have to marry her and raise children with her." The kinsman's response?

"I cannot redeem it. I might mar my own inheritance. I cannot redeem it."

And so it was, that all rights to the land and to Ruth reverted to Boaz. In that ancient culture, the symbol of a deal being finalized was the removal of a shoe. The "nearer kinsman" drew off his shoe, and handed it to Boaz saying, "Redeem all for thyself."

Never forget that the book of Ruth is a romance.

Boaz genuinely delighted in Ruth, and was thrilled at the very thought of becoming her protector and provider. He looked for a way to make it possible, while at the same time, fulfilling the law of God.

Your Kinsman Redeemer is no less thrilled with you. He looked for a way to make it possible to have a bride, while at the same time, fulfilling the law of God. He paid it all, so that you could be made dead to the law and its demands, so that you could marry another - the Lord, Christ. The law and its demands can never walk all over you again. What's more, Jesus takes delight in buying back all that was lost by your sin and idolatry. Jesus takes delight in grafting you into the family of God. Jesus takes delight in transferring all that belongs to Him, to you.

Freedom! Ruth is finally free to marry Boaz and we read that not long after, the Lord enabled her to conceive, and she gave birth to a son. For years, and for various reasons, Ruth had been barren, but her kinsman redeemer was a restorer of all that was lost, and a sustainer of all that was now his.

The book of Ruth begins with the mother-in-law, Naomi, and interestingly it ends with her as well. When baby Obed was born, he was handed to Naomi with this blessing:

4:14-15 "Blessed is the Lord who has not left you without a redeemer today, and may his name become famous in Israel."

Don't you just want to laugh? "May his name become famous in Israel"! This was a beautiful blessing, to be sure, but it was also the biggest understatement of all time. King David was Israel's most famous king. What's more, the Root and Offspring of David, Jesus Christ, is the most famous man who ever lived, and ever will live! He is famous enough to have all of human history split from before and after His advent.

"Then Naomi took the child and laid him in her lap, and became his nurse. And the neighbor women gave him a name, saying, "A son has been born to Naomi!" So they named him Obed. He is the father of Jesse, the father of David. Now these are the generations of Perez: to Perez was born Hezron, and to Hezron was born Ram, and to Ram, Amminadab, and to Amminadab was born Nahshon, and to Nahshon, Salmon, and to Salmon was born Boaz, and to Boaz, Obed, and to Obed was born Jesse, and to Jesse, David."

Obed, son of Boaz; Boaz, son of his father Salmon and (many historians believe) his mother Rahab (the youknowwhat). Boaz, like his father Salmon, must have had a "thing" for damsels in distress. I like to think that his mother Rahab (the. harlot.) instilled in him the idea that you must never judge a book by its cover. Whatever your Bible history, one thing is certain: the book of Ruth is an extraordinary, persuasive tribute to the doctrines of grace. It is also one of the best explanations of the mystery of God's sovereignty joined to human initiative, that we will ever hear.

The Prince of Preachers Charles Haddon Spurgeon was once asked, "How do you reconcile sovereignty and free will?" His answer?

"You don't need to reconcile friends."

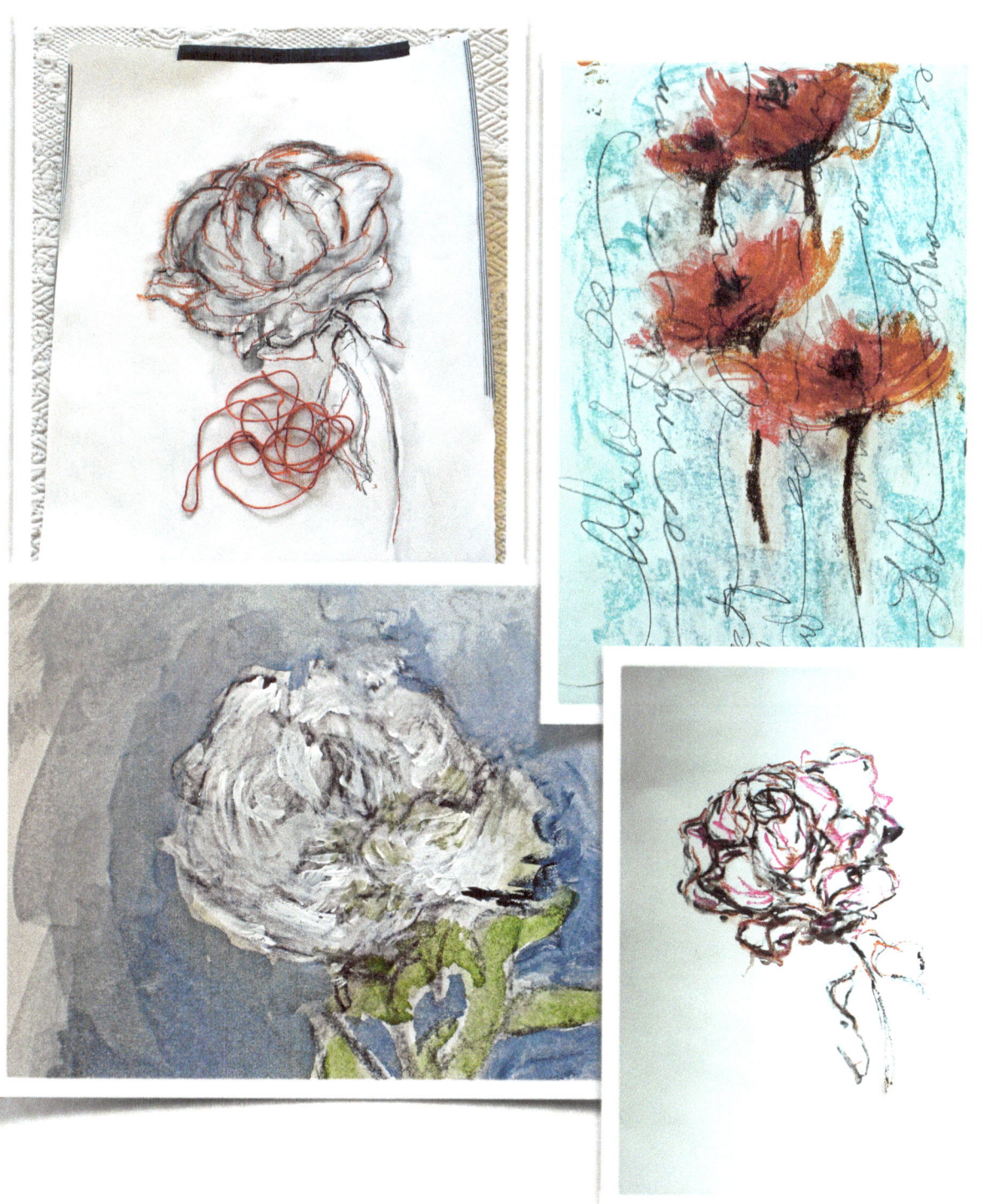

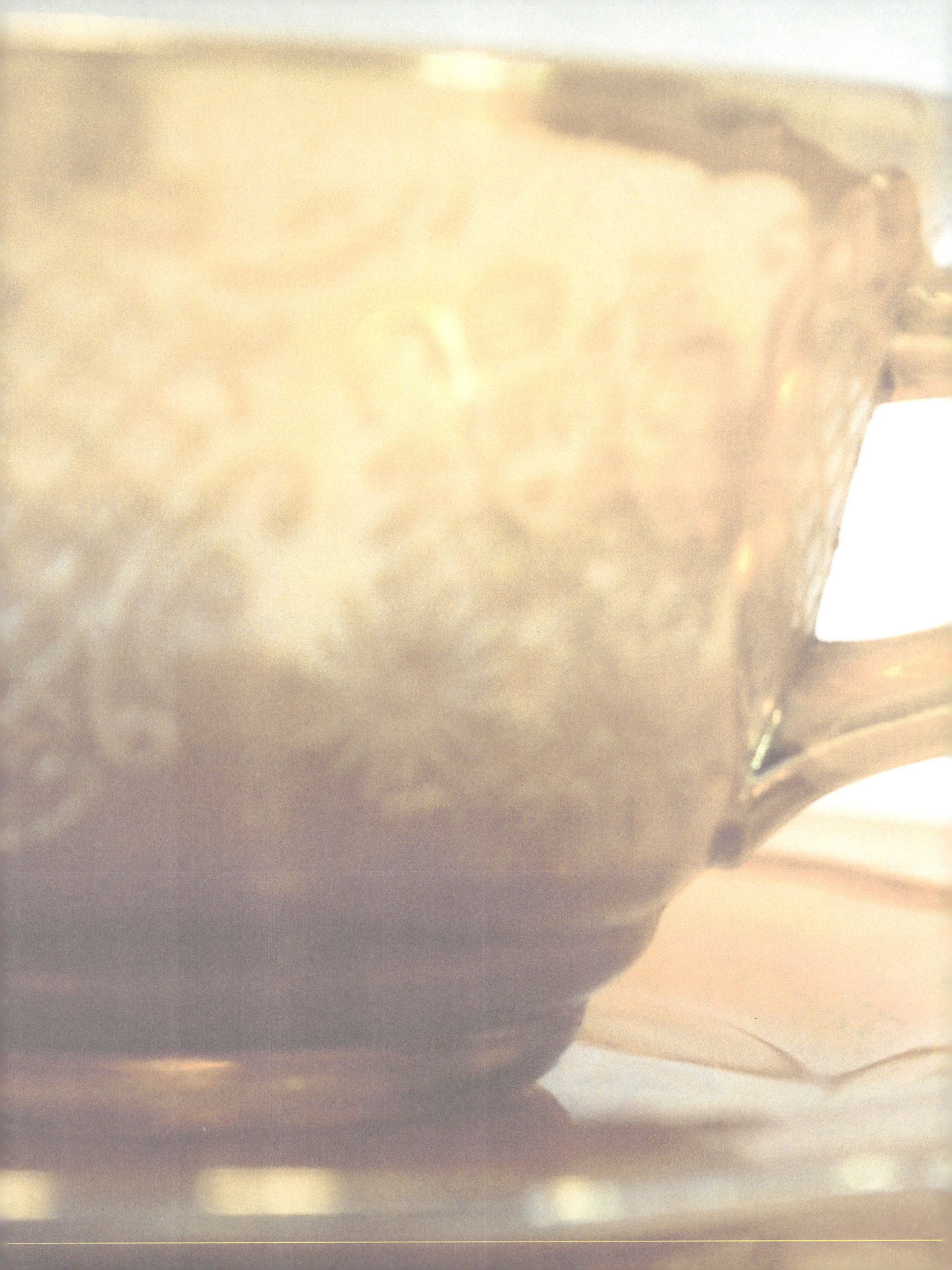

BATHSHEBA

"I AM PREGNANT."

Pour thyself a cup of hot tea
or hot, fragrant coffee
{or something fun, fruity, and with a splash of white wine}
and let's begin discussing Bathsheba.

Let's do it now, while she isn't nearby to find out that we did it

Just kidding! But isn't it interesting how
the lives of the near-us and living
should almost never be a topic of discussion
when they aren't around (it's gossip, hello!)...
...yet we are encouraged to eagerly dissect and discuss
those who have gone to their eternal reward?

I say all that to say this:
when it is us who have gone to our eternal reward,
let's hope we lived fearlessly, with initiative!
LET'S GIVE 'EM SOMETHIN' TO TALK ABOUT

Ironically, the blow-by-blow of Bathsheba's saga starts with a bath in springtime. We have Bathsheba. And we have a bath. Nothing more. It all could have been so uneventful.

"And it came to pass in an evening tide, that David rose from his bad and walked upon the roof of the kings's house: and from the roof he saw a woman washing herself; and the woman was very beautiful to look upon."

But this story began just one scant verse before, with an ill-boded, momentous _sending_. "At the time when kings go forth to battle, David sent" someone else. The rest of the tale unfolds in the same peculiar style - with everyone sending someone else, everyone messaging everyone else; it was the ancient version of texting, but with no LOL's.

It seems that we humans don't need the social media scapegoat. We cannot blame the internet or Snap Chat Stories for becoming ourselves once-removed from active participation in our own stories. We don't need technology, to depersonalize and disengage. We have been sloughing off owning our motives and mistakes in the first-person, since the garden of Eden. We've tried to remove ourselves from sin's equation way before the cold light of a screen existed.

David sent Joab to battle, instead of going himself. David sent and enquired after Bathsheba, instead of physically approaching her. David sent people to fetch Bathsheba to his bed. All the sending took place, as a way to numb the pain of responsibility or culpability. Never, in all my years of Bible study, have I seen so much sending and messaging in one chapter.

Beware what you send. Beware, when you find yourself
finding ways to not physically show up and be present in
your own life. Beware what is sent to you. Truth and
love are rarely sent. They must be carried. Somehow, in
some way, most things real and good must be conveyed,
often physically. Things merely sent can be rife with
deception. Messages passively received can be teeming
with viral distortion.

The water felt cool and comforting after an unusually warm
Jerusalem spring day. The sun was just beginning to
settle into the western horizon, and the heat of the day
was just beginning to relent, as Bathsheba took off her
outer robe. Wrapping herself in a thin bathing sheet,
then loosening her heavy hair, she sank her feet
gratefully into the pool of water, which came up past her
knees.

Just like women in all times and places everywhere, she
must have hoped her bath would soothe her aching heart as
well as her tired legs. It had not been long since she had
said goodbye to her military husband. For that matter, it
hadn't been long since her mother had said goodbye to her
father, also one of the king's mighty men of battle. It
was a way of life to Bathsheba, having been raised in a
dutiful and talented military family. Spring was the time
when kings and mighty men, otherwise known as husbands and
fathers, set out to enforce boundaries. There were many
Israelite women who would be sleeping alone this night.
She tucked her bath sheet a little tighter around her
chest.

You see, chances are very good that Bathsheba was not
bathing naked, when David spied her. Chances are, she was
mindlessly tending to herself in a ceremonial cleansing -
a common practice in Judaism.

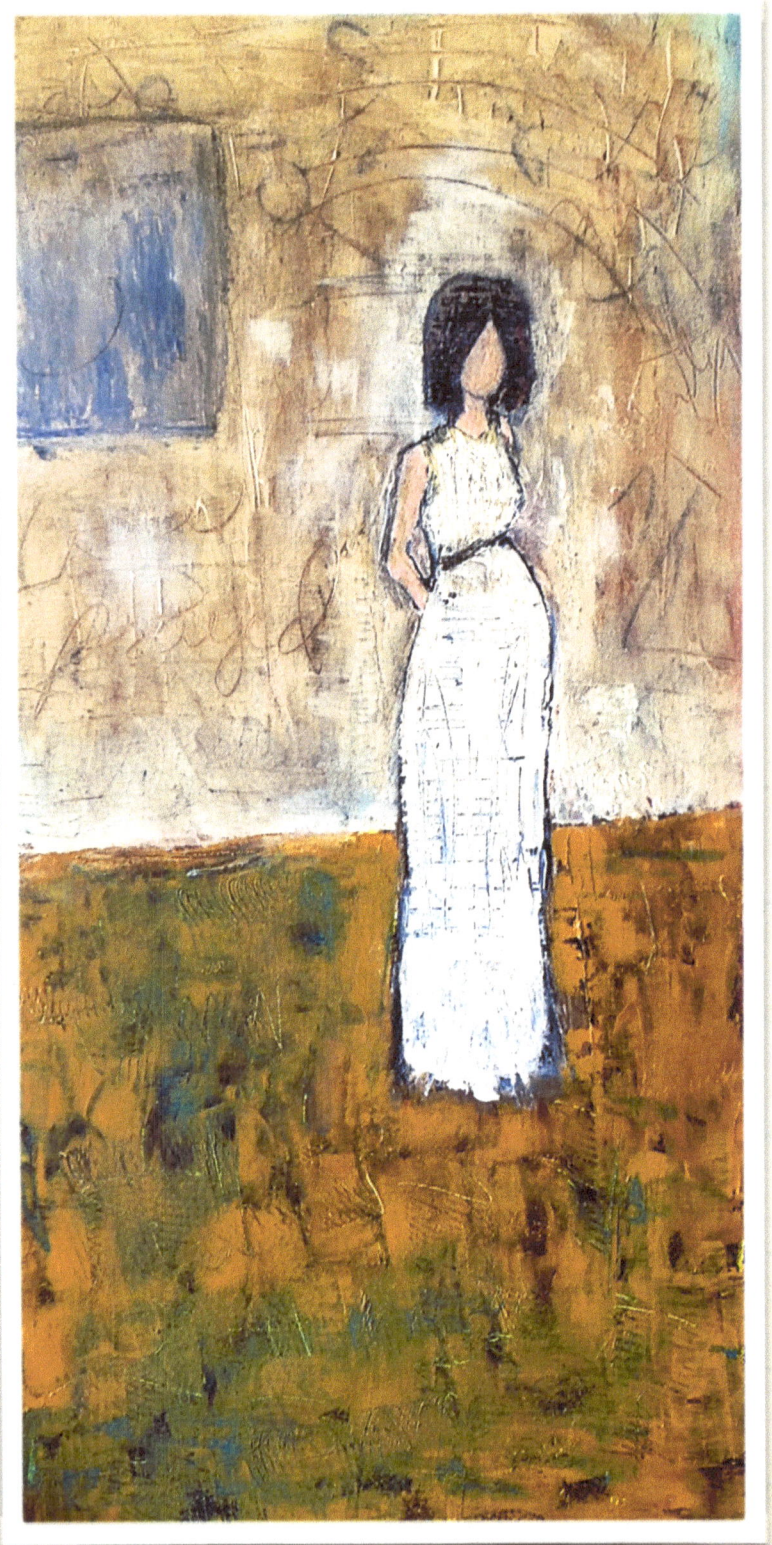

This is a mixed media
piece entitled
"Expectant".

Rendered in acrylics,
gesso, graphite,
Stabilo pencil,
willow stick and charcoal,
with accents of oil pastel.

It seems that "expecting" ~
whether a woman
has the ability to conceive,
or she does not ~

expectancy
is a
major theme in a woman's life,
bringing her either
great joy
or
untold sorrow.

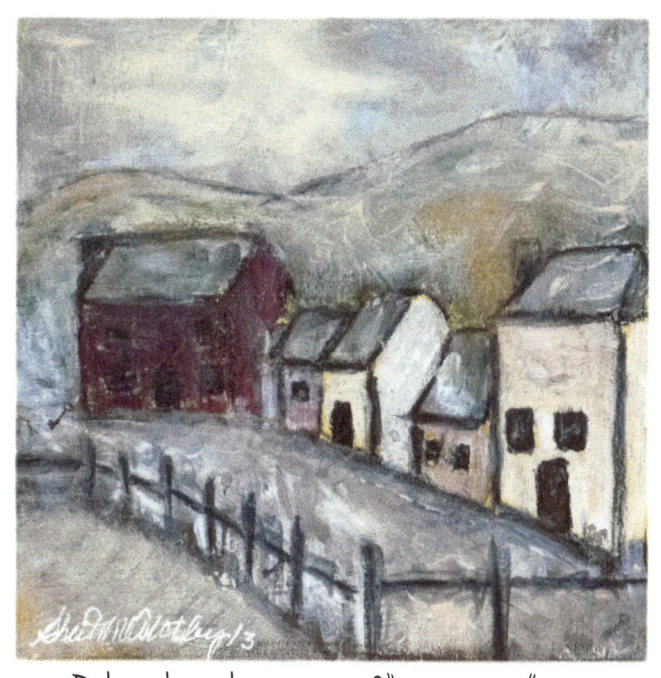

Other than the concept of "expectancy",
"Home" and "Community"
are the second most critical themes
in a woman's life, shaping all she is and all she becomes.
All these themes are prominent in my art.

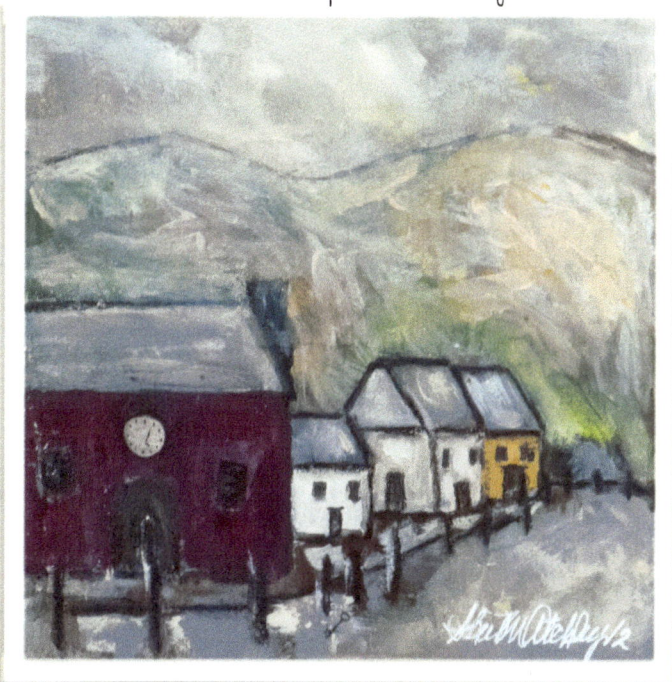

Bathsheba's private soak has forever been notoriously difficult to exegete for Bible scholars the world over. Was she being coy? Did she know the king might see her? Was she a political opportunist? An exhibitionist? Was she naked?

I've been perplexed at the numbers of learned men, good men, Godly men, who read 2 Samuel 11, and see a seductress and a social climber. I've been equally perplexed at the number of learned women, good women, Godly women, who read 2 Samuel 11, and see a helpless rape victim.

Everything feels better, when blame can be placed squarely. We like clarity, we love the convenient arraignment of potential guilt, and then the closure of consequences.

But what do you do with mixed motives? What do you do with all that is left unsaid? What do you do with the tension between guilty and not? Certainty is often obscured, tangled up in a thin bath-sheet of complex humanity; humanity that is neither wholly noble or notorious.

Ah. I think that is where art happens, though.

The most beautiful, meaningful art is never completely perfectly righteous or fully reprobate. Most educated art critics equally despise sanctimony on the one hand, and debauchery on the other. Few would frame and hang a monotone black or painfully stark white canvas. We gravitate to full and creaturely colors, replete with shades of gray. Art happens in the middle, somewhere between noble and notorious. The art that is our life hangs in the forgivable space between heaven and hell, the space where sovereignty and free will collide. The space of necessary grace.

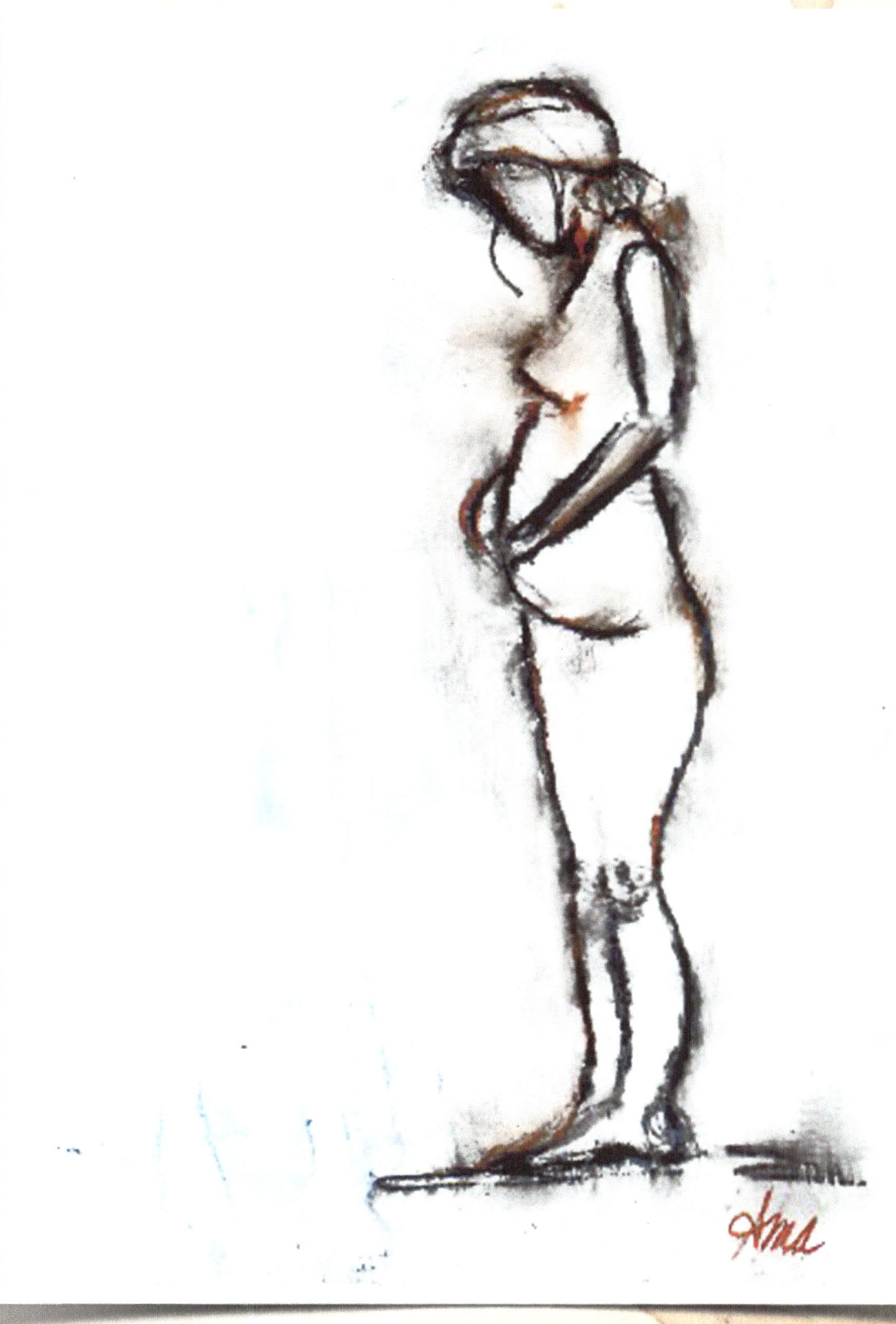

Bathsheba isn't a Tamar, Rahab or Ruth. She doesn't exhibit a flicker of the initiative that her sisters rocked their worlds with. She isn't edgy like Rahab, nor does she seem to have the assertive, hard-working loyalty and obedience of Ruth. She never comes across as desperate as a Tamar. In fact, the only thing of any consequence we really hear her say, are the three words:

"I am pregnant."

And even those words were sent as a text message. She texted the father of her child with the news. Who was Bathsheba? Now, I realize that the manners and customs of the day dictated that a message be sent. But women, even in those ancient and androcentric times, knew that "no" and "don't" could be a complete sentence. Even then, women found ways to buck the system and stick it to the man. Some even proposed marriage.

Bathsheba was the delight of every man in her life, but we see her as always, always either being sent or summoned. We never see her with the grace of gumption. We don't even know for sure how she felt about anything or anyone. The surest sense we have of her heart, is at the loss of that first born child - the baby conceived because of a springtime bath. We are certain that must have shredded Bathsheba's heart.

Even her birth-name, Bathshua, means "daughter of my prosperity". She is forever recorded in scripture as someone's daughter, someone's wife, someone's mother. She is listed in the book of Matthew, in the genealogy of Jesus, as "Uriah the Hittite's wife". She is spoken of as Uriah's wife even after her marriage to David. She is "Uriah's wife" all the way up until she loses her first child. Only when she conceives her second child with David, is she called "David's wife". Rarely is she called "Bathsheba", and even when her name is spoken, we must keep in mind, its very meaning was "someone else's daughter".

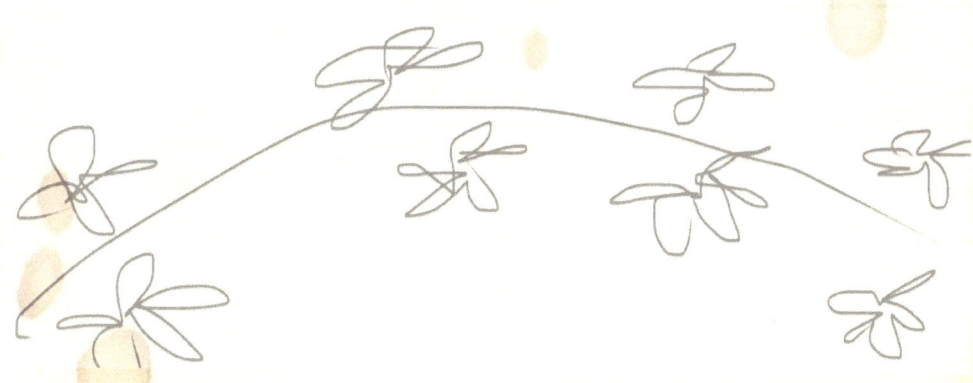

Bathsheba is comforted by David after the loss
of the first child. Nine months later, she
gives birth to Solomon-Jedidiah, and the Bible
tells us that "the Lord loved him". Her
pinnacle achievement is, in essence, that she
changed the diapers of the wisest man who ever
lived. Something tells me she didn't mind.
Bathsheba was as dutiful as she was beautiful,
and though she was one of David's many wives,
she was forever Solomon's only mother, and he
adored her.

She was daughter of / wife of / mother of.
She was beautiful. She was dutiful. She was
a grieving wife. She was a grieving mother.
She was a mother in Zion - a queen mother.
She was always being sent or summoned. She
liked baths.

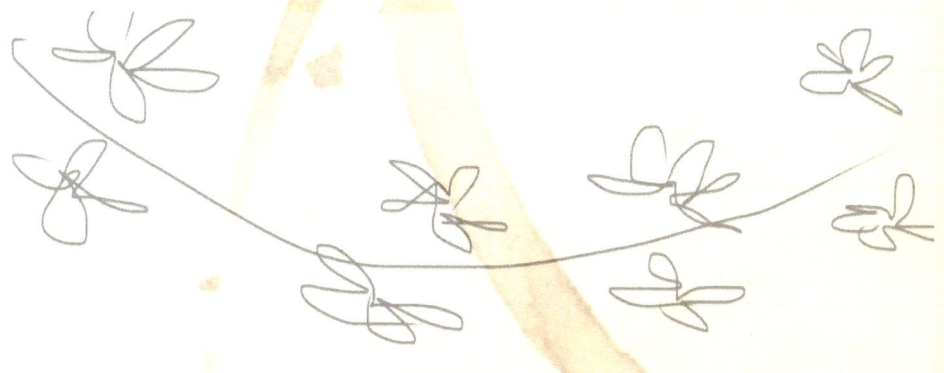

Was she a seductress? Was she a rape victim? Was she a political opportunist? Was she an innocent lamb? Was she happy with the idea of no longer being the wife of a soldier, so that she could be the wife of the king? Were her 7 days of mourning Uriah, were they 7 days of heartbreak or 7 days of going through the motions, or 7 days of mixed emotions? Did she bathe naked, or wrapped in a bath-sheet, as was also customary? And, the million-dollar question:

Did she know she was being watched, that night?

Bathsheba is a puzzle, wrapped in an enigma, shrouded with the gray smoke of mystery. There is so much we cannot know.

There is so much about this woman that is resigned to the pages of Scripture, locked up tight. Some theological feminists believe that the silence is the result of misogynist exegesis. I believe the truth is less vilifying, a little less feminist-electrifying, but incredibly satisfying.

I believe the truth is that we humans love melodrama, and we want to believe Bathsheba was either victim or victor. She was either conniving or innocent, sinner or saint. That makes for a better story, than simply being a woman with ordinary ambivalence. Mother Theresa makes for a better story than a preacher's wife who worships in spirit and truth on Sunday, yet swears on Monday morning. Rape and victimization feels like a better story line, than the fact of a girl who is swept up in the heat of a hot minute, who is as curious and aroused as the boy, who decides she doesn't want sex. . . but only after the sex happened. Who do you blame? Only truth sets you free. If the truth were told, what would the truth be? There is nothing more common, bordering on boring, than a woman who has mixed motives like the rest of us, but who just so happens to look great half-naked.

I'm not at all saying Bathsheba wasn't a victim. What I am saying, is if we stick to what is actually said in Scripture, and we leave out what was actually left unsaid, we can come away with something that sets Bathsheba apart for us, for all time.

It's precisely because we don't know and can't know for sure, that makes Bathsheba belong to all of us. Whether she was a victim or opportunist or something in between, she is given a place of honor in the genealogy of Christ. She was given the great grace of being a many times great-grandmother to God.

Rarely is a woman's life all light, or all darkness. Just like photography, the beauty happens in between the two - in the shady place of an ordinary day. Art happens in the tension between noble and notorious, so it isn't necessary to paint ourselves in extremes to have a beautiful story.

The point is, sinners and saints and women with mixed motives all get equal grace. I don't know about you, but most days I am neither martyr nor murderer. I'm neither the hunter, nor the hunted. Most days, I just want a bath. Yet, without being grafted into the vine, without being placed in the family tree of Jesus Christ, I am as without hope as any heinous perpetrator, or any voiceless victim. I am without hope precisely because I am something in the middle of sinner and saint. I am only made able to worship in spirit and truth, because there is great grace for my lukewarm soul.

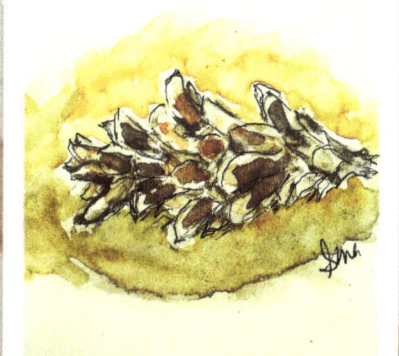

We need to tell the truth with the pages of Scripture, the same as we need to tell the truth with the events of our life - neither adding to what is really there, nor taking away from it. Jesus doesn't redeem our spin on the facts. He didn't die for our version of the story, with our fabricated innocence or borrowed guilt. We can face the truth about ourselves, even when the truth is shameful or boring. We can exchange our worn-out history, with its prosaic storyline, for His-story. We can exchange our puny visualizations of a better tomorrow, for His good plan to give us a future and a hope.

Bathsheba gave up a voice in her own life, so that she could give birth to the One who came to restore our voice. Jesus was the champion of women and their value. He elevated women, both in his ministry, and in the tenets of the New Covenant which He sealed with His own blood. In Christ, you are extraordinarily significant, and you are meant to have a voice. Men plan wars, but women plan weddings. And dear one - all of human history will culminate in a wedding. The silence and stillness of Bathsheba will become the roar and dance of the Bride!

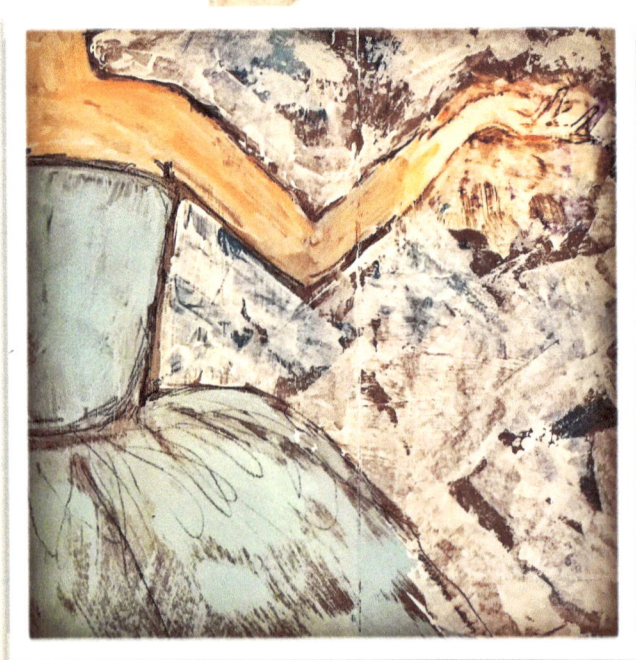

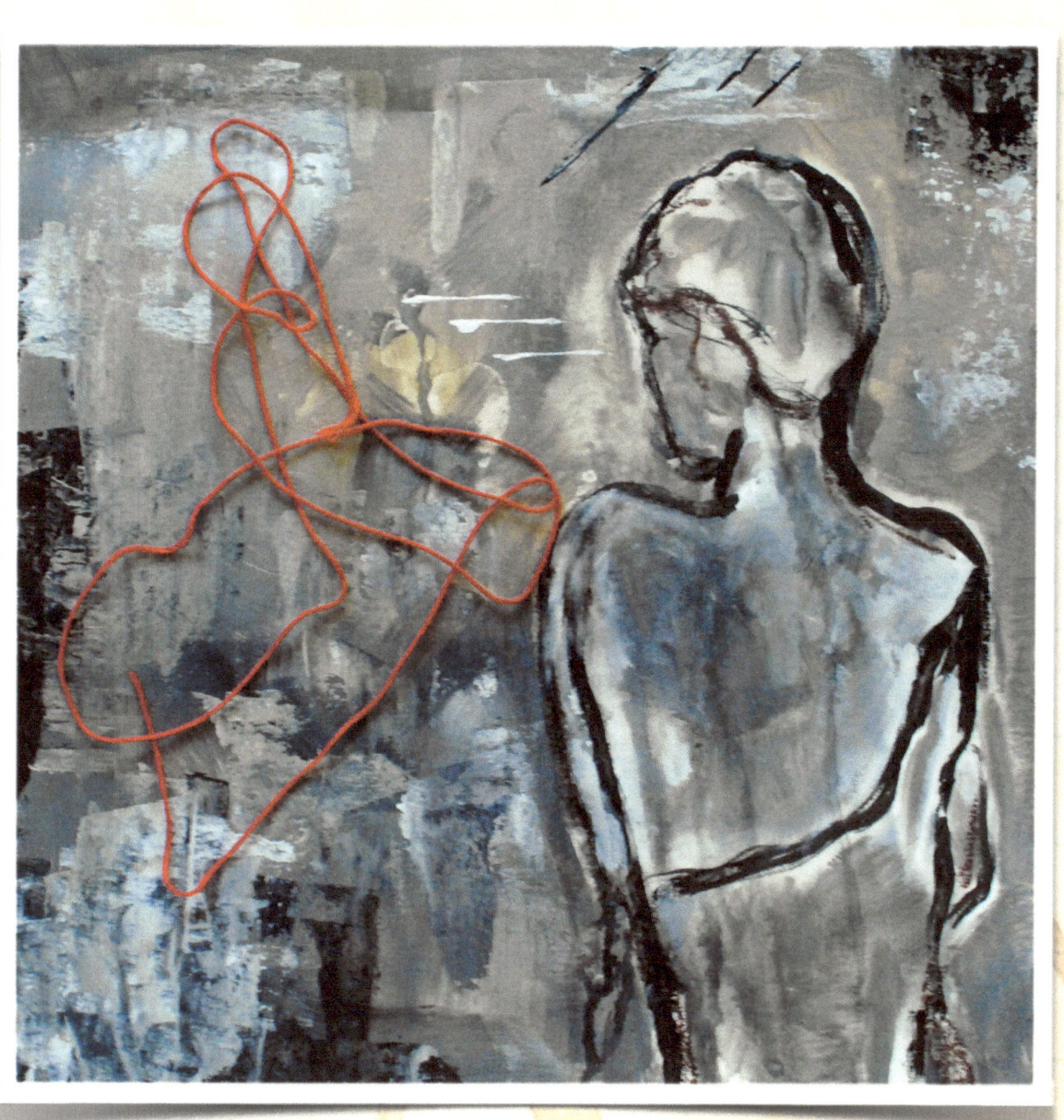

"ASKING QUESTIONS IS OF INESTIMABLE IMPORTANCE"

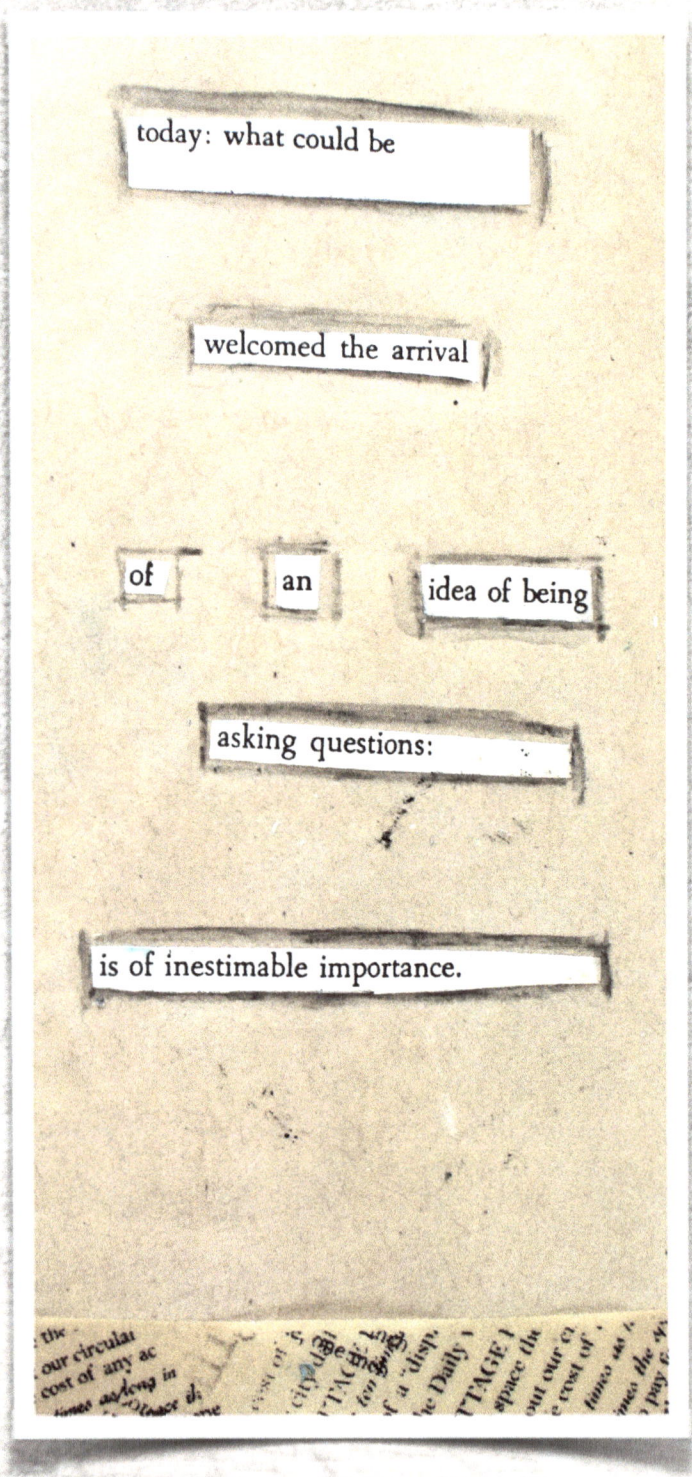

today: what could be

welcomed the arrival

of   an   idea of being

asking questions:

is of inestimable importance.

Based on the lives of Ruth and Bathsheba,
compare your present situation, in terms of kinship, with
what is possible. What does God want to do in your
relationships?:

_____
_____
_____
_____
_____
_____
_____

God is always up to a "new thing". The arrival of the
next new thing is always pending. What is yet another
important person or thing you need to welcome into your
life? How can you do this?(Do not write about who needs
to go…write about who you know needs to be welcomed in!):

_____
_____
_____
_____
_____
_____
_____

If you don't have someone to "see" you, you can "see"
yourself. Your initiative is a gift you can give
yourself, this Advent season. It is a way of seeing. It
is a fresh idea of being in the world. Choose one thing
you want to do differently, and write about it:

_____
_____
_____
_____
_____
_____

id	Julien	Quittance	Baignard
Hervieux	Lucienne	Foy	
Hèze	Louis	B. à ordre	Belliol
Honoré	Joseph	Oblig on	Davoust foy
Hory	Jean Vve née Cochin	id	Timothée
id	Victor	id	id
Houet	Aimable	Vente	Fresnaie
id	Honorine f: Mulot	Oblig on	Bouet Jean
Houssemaine	Marcel Louise Édouard	Mariage	Hervé
Huchet	Aimable et f?	Vente	à l'État
id	id	Notoriété	
id	Théophile et f?	Oblig on	Leblanc
Huet	Alexandre	Quitt.	Delaunay
id	Anne, Vve fote Vallée	Const. d'emploi	
id	Anne Vve Bayet	Mainlevée	Rouzier. Davoust
id	Jean	Consent?	
id	Michel (hér de)	Quitt.	Thommaret

week three

Mary
"Be it unto me According to Thy Word"

Here we are, week 3 already!

Please feel free to find me on
Instagram (Sheila Atchley Designs)
or Facebook (Sheila Atchley Designs)
and let me know what you think about
what you've read so far. I'd be
delighted to hear from you.

Or just shoot me an email.

Yeah. If you don't like a bit of it...

...just shoot me an email.

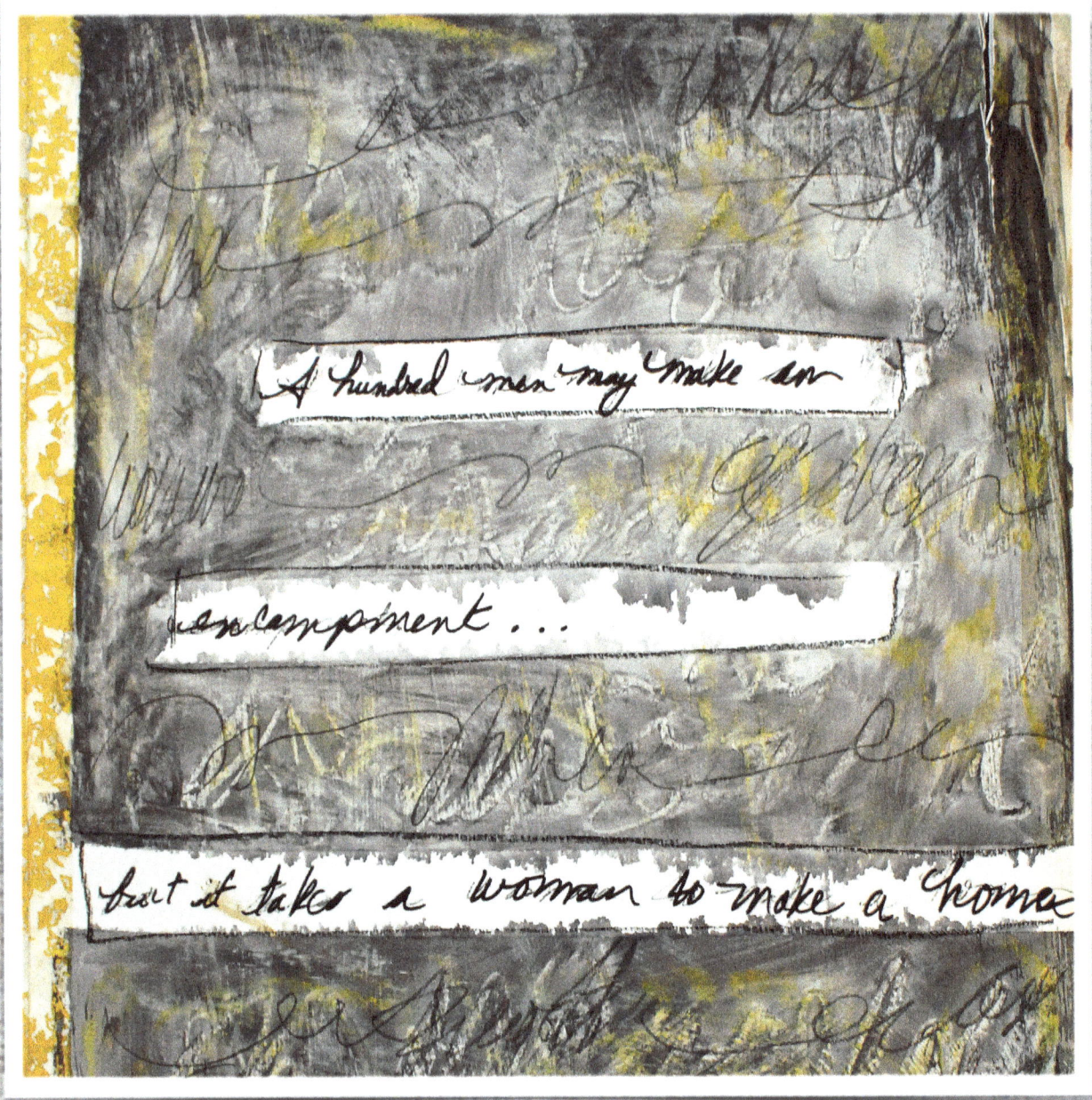

"A hundred men may make an
encampment...
but it takes a woman to make a home."

If you will do me the kindness of forbearance, I'm going to to unpack Mary in a circuitous and strange manner.

What I hope to show you is a Biblical pattern of the concept that God's sovereignty is at home with your initiative. A narrative begins for us in Joshua 17. Here, we will sink into a story...a story of the tribe of Joseph as they were beginning to take possession of their portion of the inheritance in the Promised Land.

Joshua 17: 14-18

14 The people of Joseph said to Joshua, "Why have you given us only one allotment and one portion for an inheritance? We are a numerous people, and the Lord has blessed us abundantly."

15 "If you are so numerous," Joshua answered, "and if the hill country of Ephraim is too small for you, go up into the forest and clear land for yourselves there in the land of the Perizzites and Rephaites."

16 The people of Joseph replied, "The hill country is not enough for us, and all the Canaanites who live in the plain have chariots fitted with iron, both those in Beth Shan and its settlements and those in the Valley of Jezreel."

17 But Joshua said to the tribes of Joseph—to Ephraim and Manasseh— "You are numerous and very powerful. You will have not only one allotment 18 but the forested hill country as well. Clear it, and its farthest limits will be yours; though the Canaanites have chariots fitted with iron and though they are strong, you can drive them out."

"Go up" said Joshua...who is a type of Christ. "Clear it, and it will be yours. As for those iron chariots, you can drive them out."

This tribe was being called to set their hearts higher. Asked to believe for what they could not, so that they would receive what they should not (a land that belonged to someone else). That belief had to ignite them to physical action. They had to get off their rear ends and go confront iron chariots and chop down a forest.

We see this "God's sovereignty/human initiative" pattern again and again. God wants to commit you to way bigger problems than the ones you are facing now. This is a deeply difficult challenge, and this is what keeps the blessing of believing the Gospel, (the blessing that that God wills that you prosper as your soul prospers) - this is what keeps the favor of God from becoming a false, feel-good, cotton candy prosperity gospel.

Because when you have divine FAVOR, when you are called up higher, you will end up fighting harder and working harder than ever before. God's "yes" over your life will be more difficult in some ways than the "no" would have ever been. You've heard is said, "New levels, new devils".

Few scriptures illustrate this better than Joshua 17. Joshua, our type of Christ, says, "You can do this thing. Iron weapons? That's part of receiving your promise. Iron chariots? Part of it. Intimidation? Part of it. Hard work? Part of it. Trees, boulders, obstacles everywhere? Part of obtaining your inheritance. "

Let's see this illustrated for us again...let's merge into the true story we find going on in Luke chapter 1

First, a little bit of background. This story really begins as the Old Covenant dispensation comes to its long, painful close. There are 400 years between the end of Malachi and Matthew, Mark, Luke, and John chapter 1.

Can we imagine a world where God is completely silent? For 400 years? Not a single message, almost no signs or wonders or notable provision. No strong leader with a fresh word. And the list of do's and don'ts becomes even more convoluted and complex. As we merge into this story, and ask the Holy Spirit to help us participate in it, we feel a sigh of gratitude that, in the middle of this horrible silent season, God still had precious older saints who believed God was still there, even if they could not explain His silence.

5 In the time of Herod king of Judea there was a priest named Zechariah, who belonged to the priestly division of Abijah; his wife Elizabeth was also a descendant of Aaron. 6 Both of them were righteous in the sight of God, observing all the Lord's commands and decrees blamelessly. 7 But they were childless because Elizabeth was not able to conceive, and they were both very old.

Don't you hate the "but" in your life? This couple was righteous in the sight of God, before the cross...which says a great deal about their lifestyle and their faith. But. But they were barren. They were empty, if you will.

Can I tell you? God wastes nothing. In fact, He ordains times of silence and emptiness, to prepare us for a sudden and mighty increase. Delays are not denials. It is always better to let fruit ripen before you pick it, and it is best of all to let God drop it into your outstretched hands, when the time is right. That is the sweetest fruit of all.

8 Once when Zechariah's division was on duty and he was serving as priest before God, 9 he was chosen by lot, according to the custom of the priesthood, to go into the temple of the Lord and burn incense. 10 And when the time for the burning of incense came, all the assembled worshipers were praying outside.

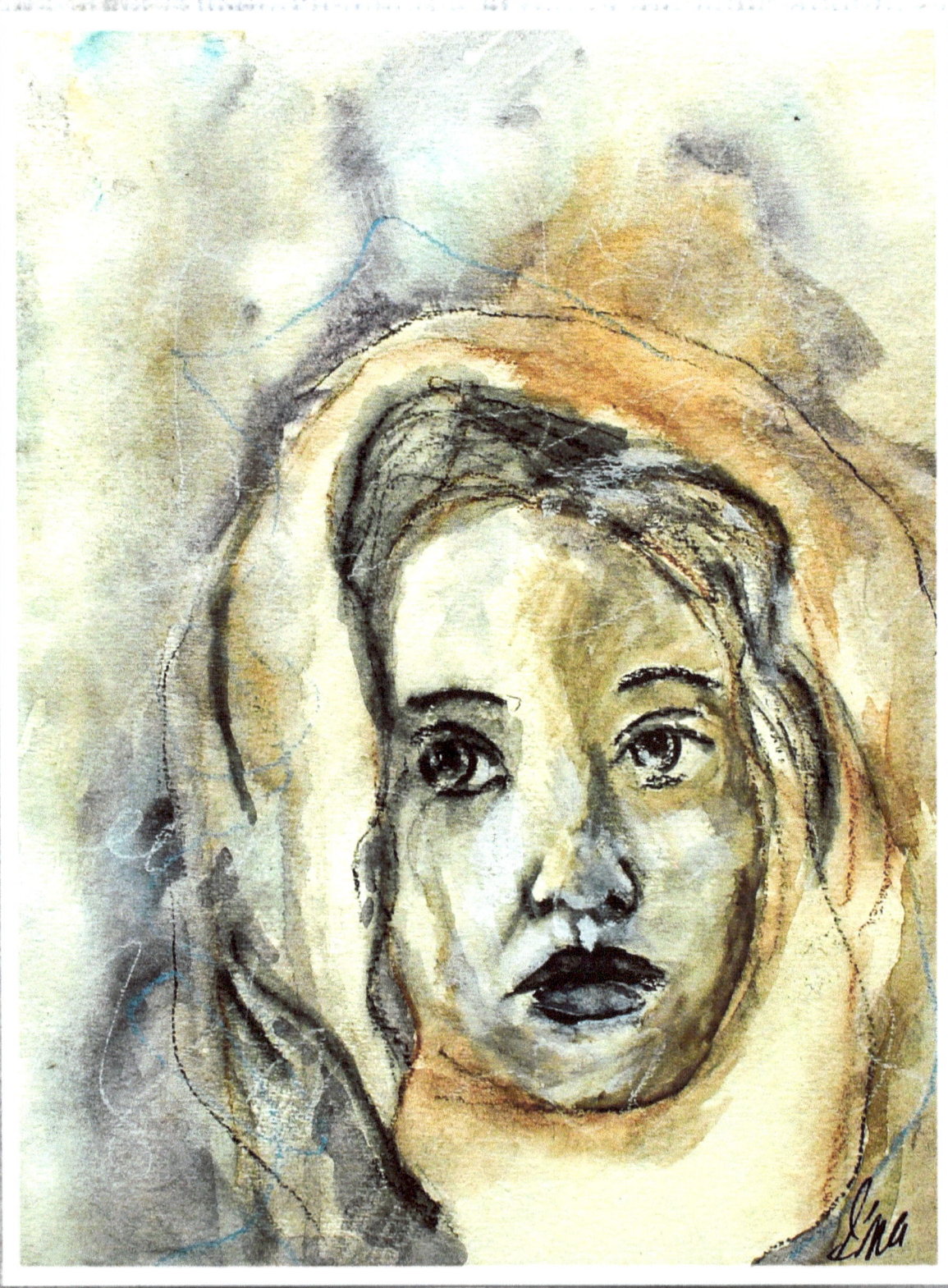

{The print on the left is entitled "Mary"}

She was so young. I often think of that ~instant~

....that moment...seconds before the angel appeared with news that would change all of us forever.

Since I'm obsessed with faces, I often wonder what her expression was, just before. I know she was alone, as I now am sometimes, in this empty-nest season.

This is that moment, as I imagine it.

None of us get advance notice. None of us are told, moments before an unexpected, life altering event, "here it comes". We all have our unanticipated appointment...we all have that one, last, final moment with our "ordinary face" before joy or pain or wonder marks us forever.

Far from being dark thoughts, I consider these ideas to be enchanting.

11 Then an angel of the Lord appeared to him, standing at the right side of the altar of incense. 12 When Zechariah saw him, he was startled and was gripped with fear. 13 But the angel said to him: "Do not be afraid, Zechariah; your prayer has been heard.

Two things to understand here: 1) You have to come to grips with fear before you can lay hold of faith. 2) The other is that personal prayers matter in history. There were lots of priests and people praying in Israel. But Gabriel says to Zechariah, "YOUR prayer has been heard." We'll develop this more in a moment.

Your wife Elizabeth will bear you a son, and you are to call him John. 14 He will be a joy and delight to you, and many will rejoice because of his birth, 15 for he will be great in the sight of the Lord. He is never to take wine or other fermented drink, and he will be filled with the Holy Spirit even before he is born. 16 He will bring back many of the people of Israel to the Lord their God. 17 And he will go on before the Lord, in the spirit and power of Elijah, to turn the hearts of the parents to their children and the disobedient to the wisdom of the righteous—to make ready a people prepared for the Lord."

God had not only been silent for 400 years, but He had also permitted this couple to walk through a very painful, intimate heartache - SO THAT He could do something big in the earth. Tucked into the answer to this couple's prayer was the fulfillment of a 400 year old prophecy back in the days of Malachi. The answer to the prayers of one, became the answer to the prayers of many. God's economy is past finding out. Never be reluctant to bring your personal needs before Him. The return of your prodigal might be for bigger reasons than you know. The success of your business may have a lot more to do with the advancement of God's plan in the earth than you realize. What blesses and heals you will always, and at the very least, positively affect those closest to you.

But here comes the sad-trumpet-sound, "womp-womp" moment:

18 Zechariah asked the angel, "How can I be sure of this? I am an old man and my wife is well along in years."

Notice he did not say, "How shall these things happen?" He says, "How can I be sure of this?"

Um, dude. There is a giant angel standing in front of you. Can you at least adjust the setting of your heart to believe and be sure that you are not having a normal day?

19 The angel said to him, "I am Gabriel. I stand in the presence of God, and I have been sent to speak to you and to tell you this good news. 20 And now you will be silent and not able to speak until the day this happens, because you did not believe my words, which will come true at their appointed time."

When you don't adjust your heart to believe, you risk losing your voice.

21 Meanwhile, the people were waiting for Zechariah and wondering why he stayed so long in the temple. 22 When he came out, he could not speak to them. They realized he had seen a vision in the temple, for he kept making signs to them but remained unable to speak.

23 When his time of service was completed, he returned home. 24 After this his wife Elizabeth became pregnant and for five months remained in seclusion. 25 "The Lord has done this for me," she said. "In these days he has shown his favor and taken away my disgrace among the people."

26 In the sixth month of Elizabeth's pregnancy, God sent the angel Gabriel to Nazareth, a town in Galilee, 27 to a virgin pledged to be married to a man named Joseph, a descendant of David. The virgin's name was Mary. 28 The angel went to her and said, "Greetings, you who are highly favored! The Lord is with you."

29 Mary was greatly troubled at his words and wondered what kind of greeting this might be.

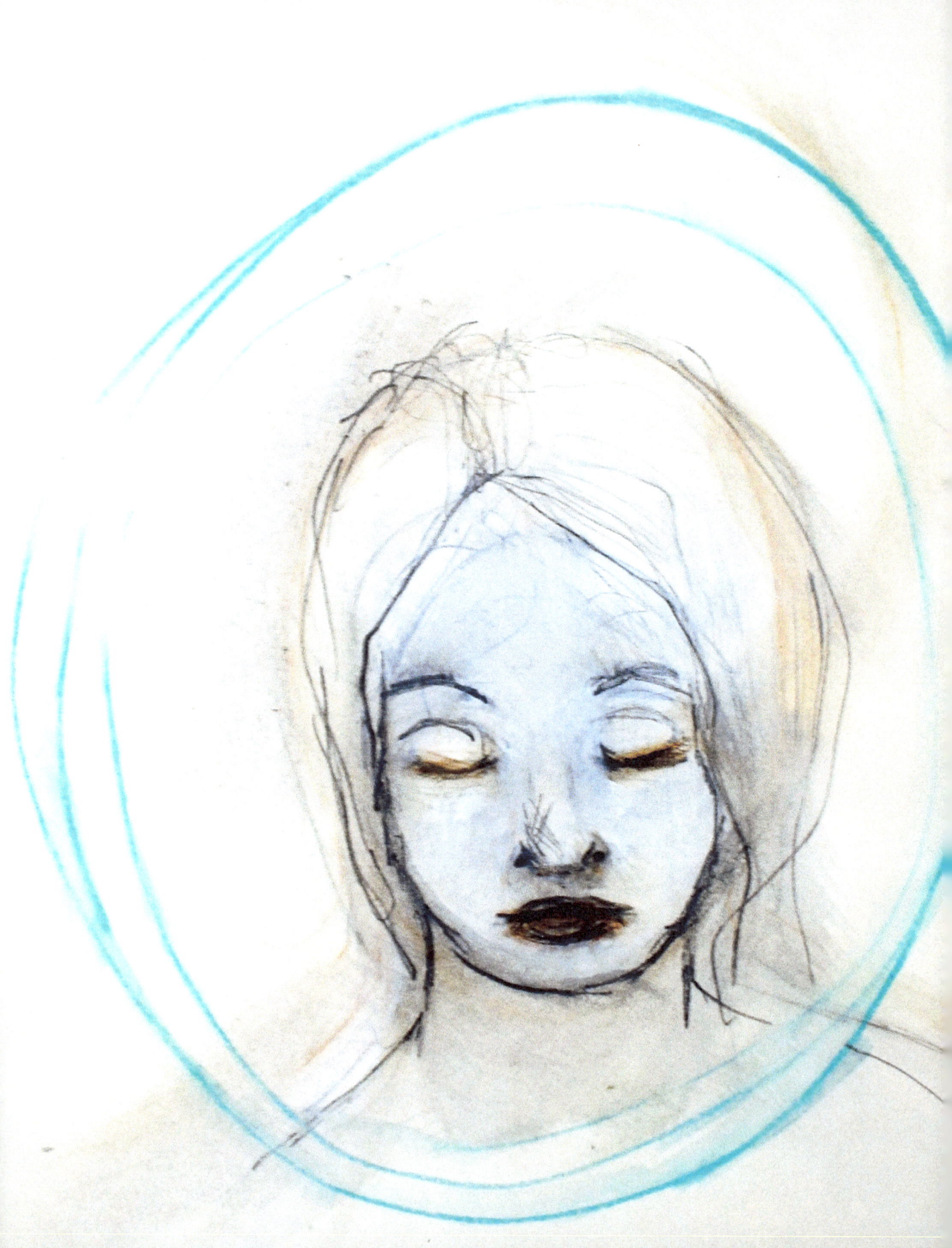

A better word here would be "perplexed". Mary was greatly
perplexed by these words. She wondered at this greeting
because first, women were not favored...ever. Women were
property. And she was but a poor young woman, betrothed
to an equally poor man, of little influence.

She had no clue that God's eye had been on her all her
life.

30 But the angel said to her, "Do not be afraid, Mary; you have found favor with God. 31 You
will conceive and give birth to a son, and you are to call him Jesus. 32 He will be great and will
be called the Son of the Most High. The Lord God will give him the throne of his father David,
33 and he will reign over Jacob's descendants forever; his kingdom will never end."

34 "How will this be," Mary asked the angel, "since I have never known a man?"

Notice Mary's question was not, "How can I be sure this is
God?" but rather, "Ok. I hear and believe what you
say...but how will it happen, since I have never known a
man?"

35 The angel answered, "The Holy Spirit will come on you, and the power of the Most High will
overshadow you. So the holy one to be born will be called[b] the Son of God. 36 Even Elizabeth your
relative is going to have a child in her old age, and she who was said to be unable to conceive is in her
sixth month. 37 For no word from God will ever fail."

38 "I am the Lord's servant," Mary answered. "May your word to me be fulfilled." Then the angel
left her.

39 At that time Mary AROSE.

Oh, please hear me when I say:

Gabriel's message, this pronouncement of heaven's favor, brought with it a lot of reproach and misunderstanding. God's favor on Mary instantly committed her, young and inexperienced as she was, to a whole new set of problems.

These new problems were far, far bigger than those she faced before she was made aware of being so favored. How many of you have been asking for favor? Are you ready to trade in your present issues for brand new, bigger and better ones? Because that's part of favor. That's part of obtaining your inheritance, part of increase. That's part of being called higher. This is where God's sovereignty is at home with your initiative.

Like Mary, we must find it in our heart to say, "Be it unto me according to Thy Word." Like Mary we will have to believe what we cannot, in order to receive what we should not, and be ignited to action.   Mary got UP off her backside. She got off her backside to obey God in seeking out likeminded, face-to-face, heart-to-heart fellowship. Gabriel didn't tell her about Elizabeth to just be chatting or telling her secrets, or to be saying "Girrrrrl. Did you know. . .?".

The Lord, through His angel, was directing Mary into fellowship. You have to know this: when you are birthing something big, you need likeminded women in your life.

Mary arose and hurried to a town in the hill country of Judea, 40 where she entered Zechariah's home and greeted Elizabeth. 41 When Elizabeth heard Mary's greeting, the baby leaped in her womb, and Elizabeth was filled with the Holy Spirit. 42 In a loud voice she exclaimed: "Blessed are you among women, and blessed is the child you will bear! 43 But why am I so favored, that the mother of my Lord should come to me? 44 As soon as the sound of your greeting reached my ears, the baby in my womb leaped for joy. 45 Blessed is she who has believed that the Lord would fulfill his promises to her!"

Here we see Elizabeth doing what all women who are truly filled with the spirit will do: she opened her mouth and spoke the mind of God. Her heart was filled with God's agenda, and out of her heart, her mouth spoke.

Tucked into her words, I discover the blessing that all pregnant grandmothers (like me) need to be declaring over the younger daughters of Zion:

Beautiful Daughter, you are BLESSED when you BELIEVE.

Mary's Song

46 And Mary said:
"My soul glorifies the Lord
47   and my spirit rejoices in God my Savior,
48 for he has been mindful
    of the humble state of his servant.
From now on all generations will call me blessed,
49   for the Mighty One has done great things for me—
    holy is his name.
50 His mercy extends to those who fear him,
    from generation to generation.
51 He has performed mighty deeds with his arm;
    he has scattered those who are proud in their inmost thoughts.
52 He has brought down rulers from their thrones
    but has lifted up the humble.
53 He has filled the hungry with good things
    but has sent the rich away empty.
54 He has helped his servant Israel,
    remembering to be merciful
55 to Abraham and his descendants forever,
    just as he promised our ancestors."
56 Mary stayed with Elizabeth for about three months and then returned home.

I will be 50 years old, by the time this book reaches your heart.

Did you know I'm pregnant?

Did you know YOU are pregnant?

To the youngest girl reading this book, if you will allow me poetic license: you are pregnant with divine destiny.

To the oldest woman, into whose hands this book is "hap to light": if you are full of God's agenda growing inside of you, if you are full of the seed of His word, you are expectant.

To every woman, past menopause, who was never able to have a child, to every woman who has been barren, God has heard your cry, and you are nevertheless expectant!

To the young mama of many, adopted or not, please don't shoot me. . .you're expectant.

May we call out to one another. May our singing span the generational gap. SING WITH ME. Rejoice with me.

Because regardless of age, we can be the channel for new things to spring forth in the Kingdom of God. I believe this is the feminine version of the prophecy we read at the end of Malachi: that at the end of this long, hard, 400 years of silence, the hearts of the fathers would be turned to the sons, and the sons to the fathers. The hearts of the grandmothers and mothers will be turned to the daughters, and the daughters to the mothers and grandmothers.

Women of all generations will come together in these amazing days. We are so much more powerful together than we are alone.

Mary and Elizabeth.
I don't often draw my Great Women of the Faith with their head coverings on.
There's no theological reason why - I simply want to see what their hair looked like.

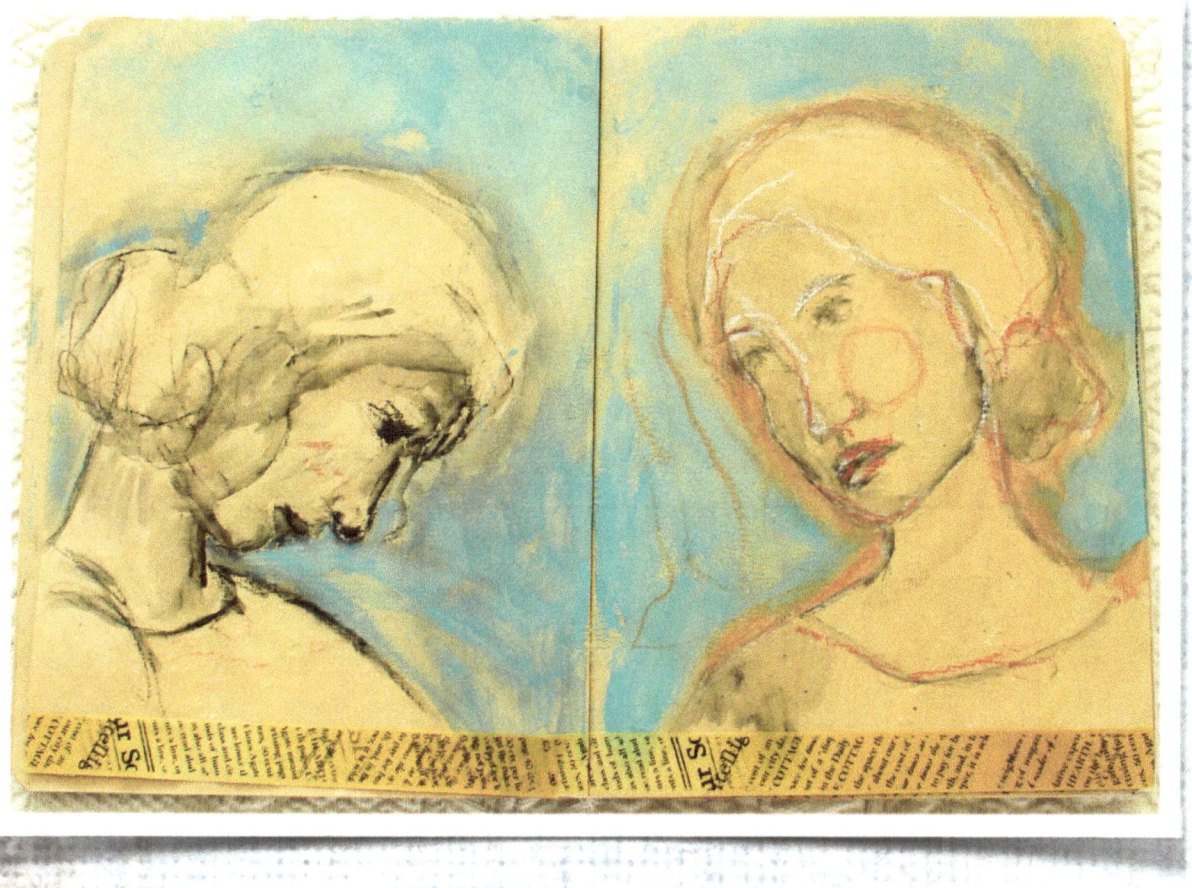

"ASKING QUESTIONS IS OF INESTIMABLE IMPORTANCE"

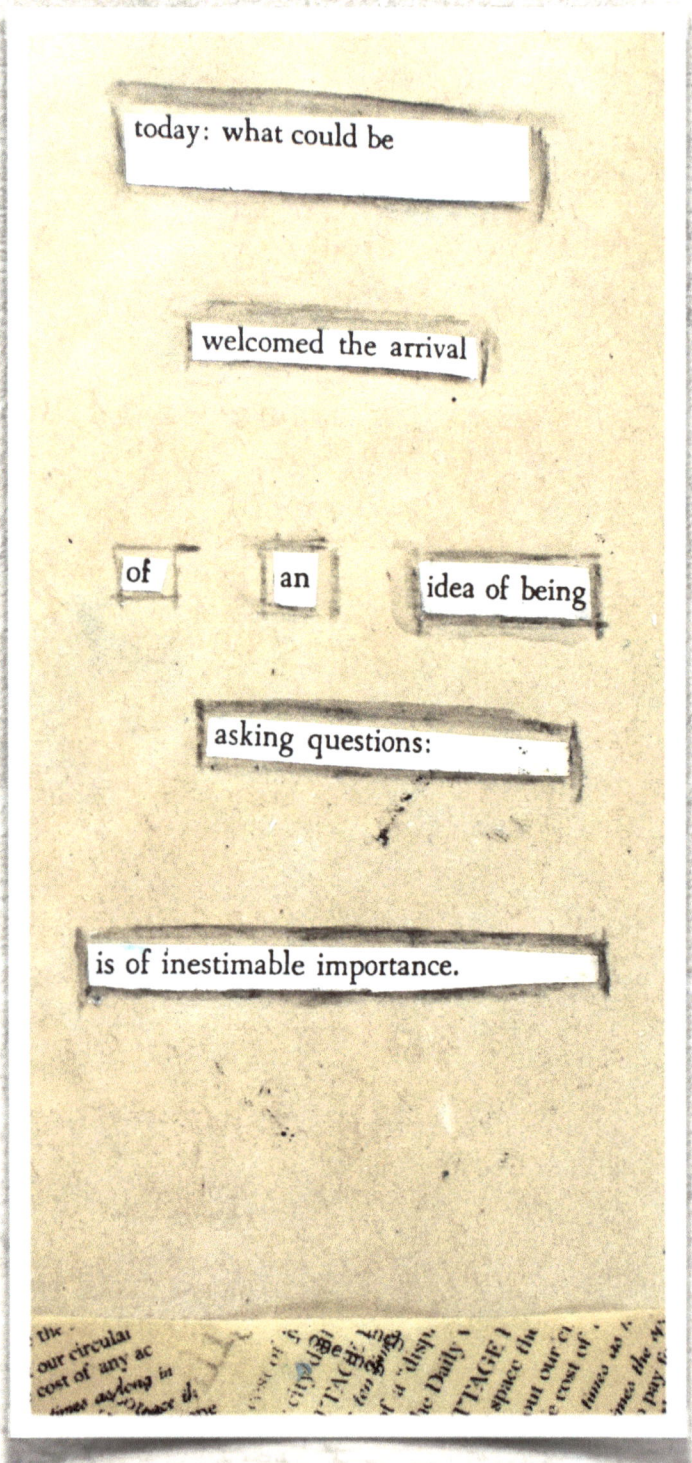

today: what could be

welcomed the arrival

of   an   idea of being

asking questions:

is of inestimable importance.

Based on the life of Mary, compare your present situation with what is possible. Remember to say, "Be it unto me according to Thy word!":

_____
_____
_____
_____
_____
_____
_____

God is always up to a "new thing". The arrival of the next new thing is always pending. What is another thing you need to welcome into your life? Has Mary given you any fresh insight?(Do not write about what needs to go… write about what you want to see ushered in!)

_____
_____
_____
_____
_____
_____
_____

Your initiative is a gift you can use to bless others, like Elizabeth blessed Mary. It is a way of seeing. It is a fresh idea of being in the world. Choose someone you want to bless, and write about it:

_____
_____
_____
_____
_____
_____

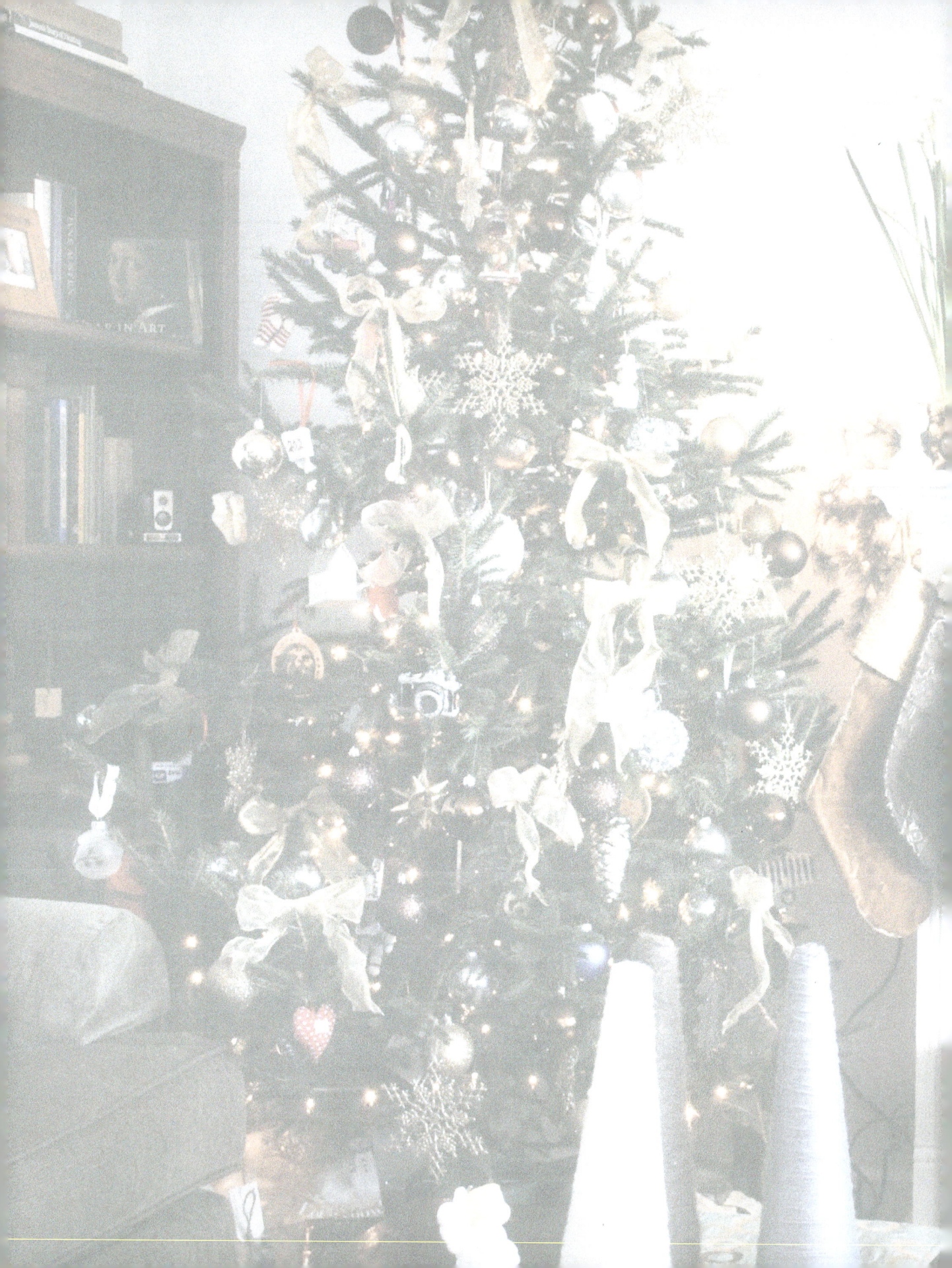

week four

YOU

"BLESSED IS SHE WHO BELIEVES"

It's almost Christmas!

The whole idea of Advent,
this way of marking time . . .

. . . of letting the anticipation build . . .

it just never gets old, does it?

We are still of those who wait
for the (second) coming of the King.

Oh, my friend!
"Who is this King of Glory?"

The world is still asking that question.
May they see Him in YOU.

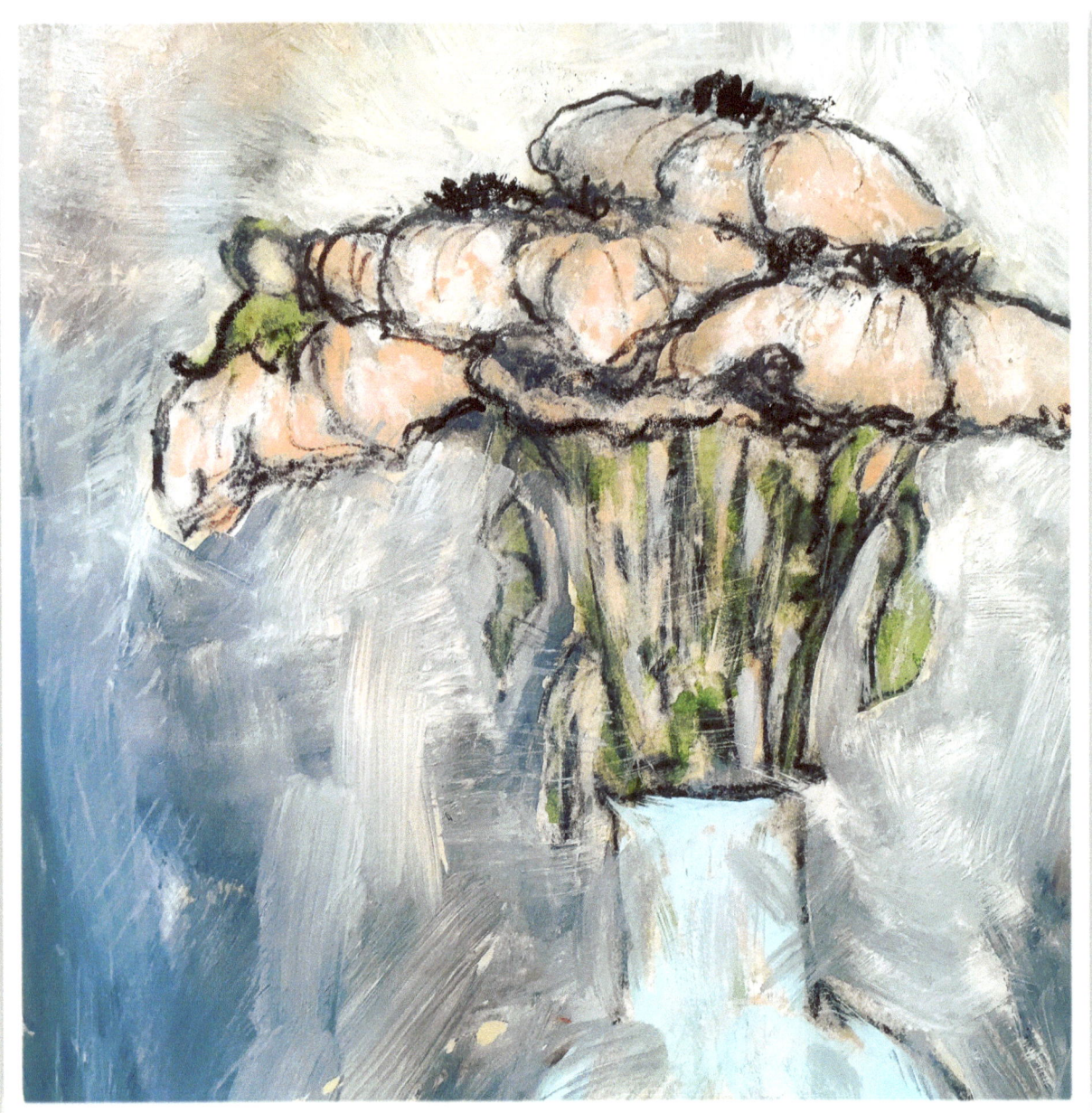

A page from my art journal. Have you ever painted a flower that you know for a fact does not exist...but you are equally sure it SHOULD exist?
That is how I felt about this bouquet.
Rendered in acrylic in shades of robin's egg blue, warm gray, sap green, titanium white, and salmon pink,
I first drew the flowers and vase in with stabilo pencil.
I finished this off with hits of a wide, dry brush loaded with titanium white paint.

God wants, this Christmas season, to show you how to set your heart on a new and higher setting. He wants to ignite your soul, and call you to action.

Why is it we can hear encouraging and inspiring words, and wake up the next day and be completely unmotivated or even depressed? Why do some things not stick with us? Because of the setting of our heart. God wants our hearts set at their highest setting. When I was younger, I had big hair. Different hair. Hair that would hold a curl mercilessly. I would set it with heat rollers, spray those rollers while they were still in my hair, and when I took my hair down, you could pull on one of those curls all day long, but it would spring right back to the way it had been set.

In your home, you have a thermostat. You have it set. If the temperature falls below that set point, your heat kicks on. If it goes above that set point, the air kicks on.

Your heart has a setting. Each of us has a different heart setting, for the most part. I'm here to tell you that other people cannot set your heart. Circumstances cannot ultimately set your heart. The devil cannot set your heart. And God <u>will not</u> set your heart. It is your awesome responsibility and privilege to set your heart.

The setting of your heart can be defined as that frustration point where you begin to level off in your experience. We all have a slightly different place where that begins to happen to us. And God wants to set our hearts higher. I also happen to believe that when a group of people will willingly set their hearts as high as they will go, crazy things like expectancy, freedom, rushing mighty winds and tongues of fire can begin to happen.

One way we can re-set our heart, is to take note of how
we approach the Scriptures. They are more than
inspiration, more than information, more than self-help,
more than even a "love letter" to us. (I just heard the
moo'ing of a Great Sacred Cow...my apologies for shooting
it.)

God's word is a love letter, to be sure, but it is more.
God's word is, itself, alive and active and
accomplishing much in the earth. It is affecting much
more than my own little world, and in fact it can open
my heart to much broader horizons, if I will allow it.
We can adjust the posture of our heart to be one of deep
awe and healthy fear, asking God to speak to us, and
whatever He says to us, we will do.

That's the thing.

We will do what we see Him doing.

As we broke open this word together, these recent weeks
of Advent, let's be careful both how we HEAR and how we
READ. To echo the profound insight of Eugene Peterson
in his incredible book _Eat This Book_, I will also say,
in my own words, that we aren't looking for principles
to snatch up and apply to our own aspirations. We
aren't even looking to have our needs met. We aren't
even looking for something relevant to our everyday
lives, as though our every day lives are the fundamental
reality. No. Christ and His Kingdom...His
church...these are the fundamental realities. The Holy
Spirit is with you and I right now to show us Jesus, and
to reveal to us all that is ours through Him.

We treat the Bible as though it were a Costco parking
lot, where we pull into the most convenient parking
space, and go obtain what will meet our needs for the
week.

Now. I welcome you to treat this devotional in just
that way. Peruse it, season after season I hope, and
grab what you need, and go your way. Let me be your 7-
Eleven. Let me be your Costco. I'm good with that.
All devotionals are perfect for that.

But not the Bible.
The Bible is
stories of true
history. It is
revelation. We
enter into story.
We are merge into a
flow of history and
present time not
determined by us,
not for our
personal agenda,
but something in
time and eternity
in which we are
invited to
participate. I hope
I've shared stories
with you from a
book that is alive
and active, which
is so different
from books that can
be handled,
analyzed, or used
for our own
purposes. God's
word is revelatory
and personal, rather
than merely informational.

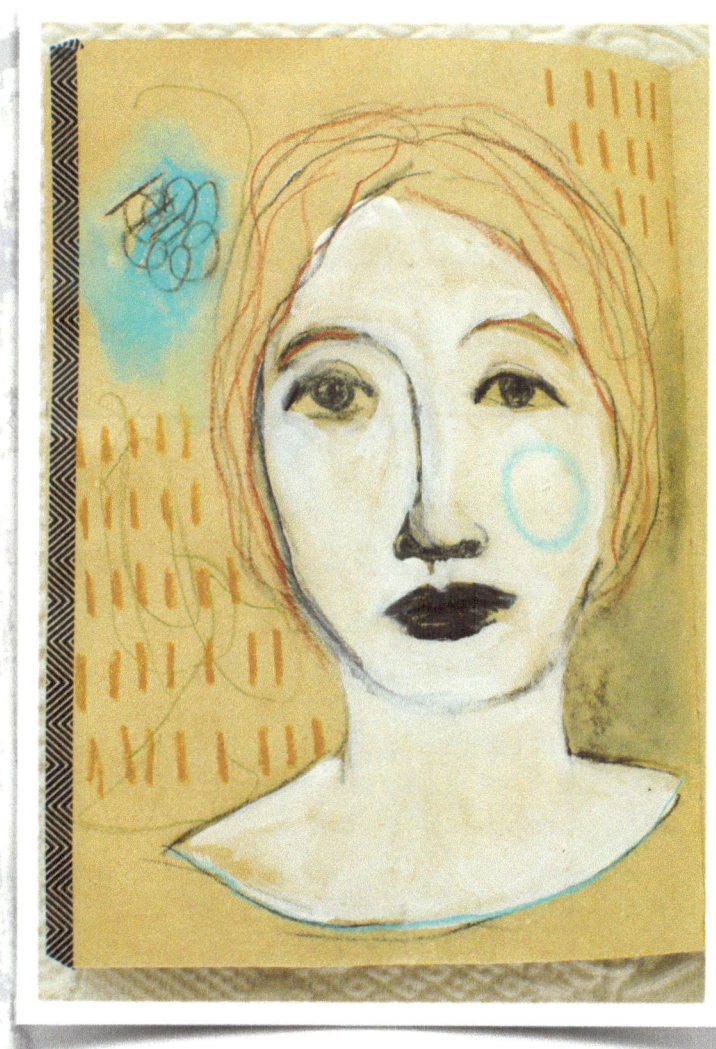

We are God's gift to this world, much in the same way Christ was God's gift to us. God became flesh in the face of Jesus. "The word was made flesh and dwelt among us."

The word is made flesh again, in a sense, when you and I receive the Scriptures and act on them. God once again becomes flesh in the form of you and I, "His body".

Advent isn't over in January! We await His second appearing, His second advent, and this world waits for you and me to manifest His heart in the earth.

The incarnation is not over. The incarnation perpetuates itself with the conversion of each new believer in Jesus. He is still Immanuel. The incarnation perpetuates itself with the ordinary acts of each woman whose heart surrenders to His Lordship.

Just as God delighted to manifest His God-ness through the medium of a woman's birth canal, being born in a barn, God delights in manifesting His God-ness through my weak human-ness.

The fact that He has taken up His abode in your temple sanctifies you! It makes you incredibly special.

When you purchase a Christmas gift, or make a Christmas present, you practice a form of sanctification! Of all the tea towels or ties in the world, you pick one tie especially suited for dad (or the tea towel for your sister). You make sure that it is not dirty, and you place it in a perfectly sized box, nest it in fluffy tissue, wrap the box in carefully chosen paper, and place a ribbon around the whole thing.

You have just sanctified a common tie or tea towel!

We do it with shirts, toys, slippers, and cookies. All manner of ordinary things become "sanctified" at Christmas. We take the common, we choose it, clean it up, fix it up, or create it from nothing. We lovingly package it up, and the very act of presenting it as a love-gift makes that common thing uncommon. God did that with the human soul.

To view the process of sanctification as grim, is to miss the point entirely. It is to wonder why "Jesus calls us kids weak butts", or to wonder why the "holy infant so tender and mild sleeps in heavenly PEAS."

Sanctification is a happy process, initiated and completed by God Himself. Everyone cleans up for a party! If you love the holidays (holy-days) you decorate for them. No one attends a wedding celebration in their gardening overalls. Everyone loves a gift.

Christ in me, the Bible says, is hope of glory! Christ in me, getting me ready for a future wedding celebration - the marriage supper of the Lamb. Christ in me, God's gift to the world on an ordinary Wednesday.

Don't think for a moment that if the vessel contains Christ within, that the earthen vessel isn't a little bit amazing, and also sanctified. You are a hint of the treasure you contain.

To take the idea a little further, the command to "remember" and sanctify the Sabbath has not been revoked. Days are common. There are 365 of them in a year, and countless numbers of them have come and gone since day 1 of creation.

But repeatedly, we are asked to sanctify one day out of every seven. We are to put that day in a box, so to speak, apart from all the others, and we are to adorn it, decorate it, cherish it, and rest on it. To rest is another way of saying, ". . .relax. . .enjoy." Of all the days in the week, this one is different.

Of all the neckties in the world, this one is for dad. Of all the Christmas trees available, this one holds the honor of being adorned with things precious to your family. Common things like ties and trees are sanctified by our love.

These are thrilling thoughts, evoking warm emotion - not grim, joy-less duties. Thus, sanctification plays out in your life. Thus, you enter into His rest. Since the incarnation is not yet over, Jesus is the gift that keeps on giving, and your life is a gift as well.

You are the earthen vessel, the special box containing His Unspeakable Gift. Christ has already sanctified you, if you are His! Containing Him, and being one of His gifts to the world, is what sanctifies you, by grace through faith. This is what celebration is all about. Believe it. Because "blessed is she who believes"!

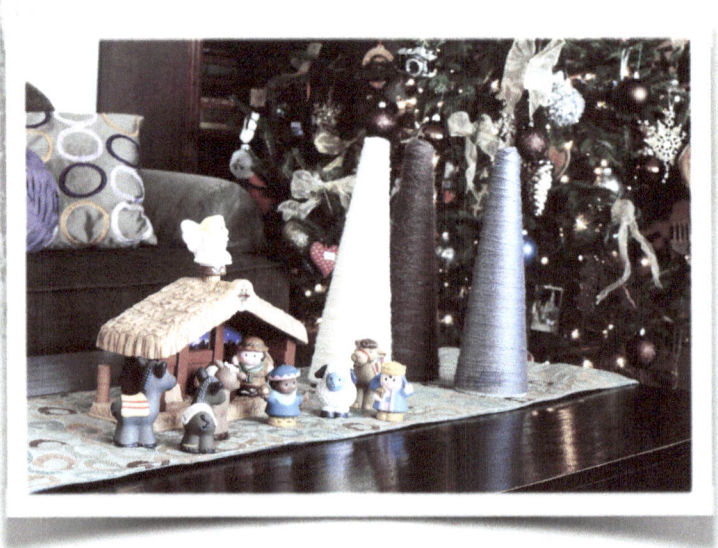

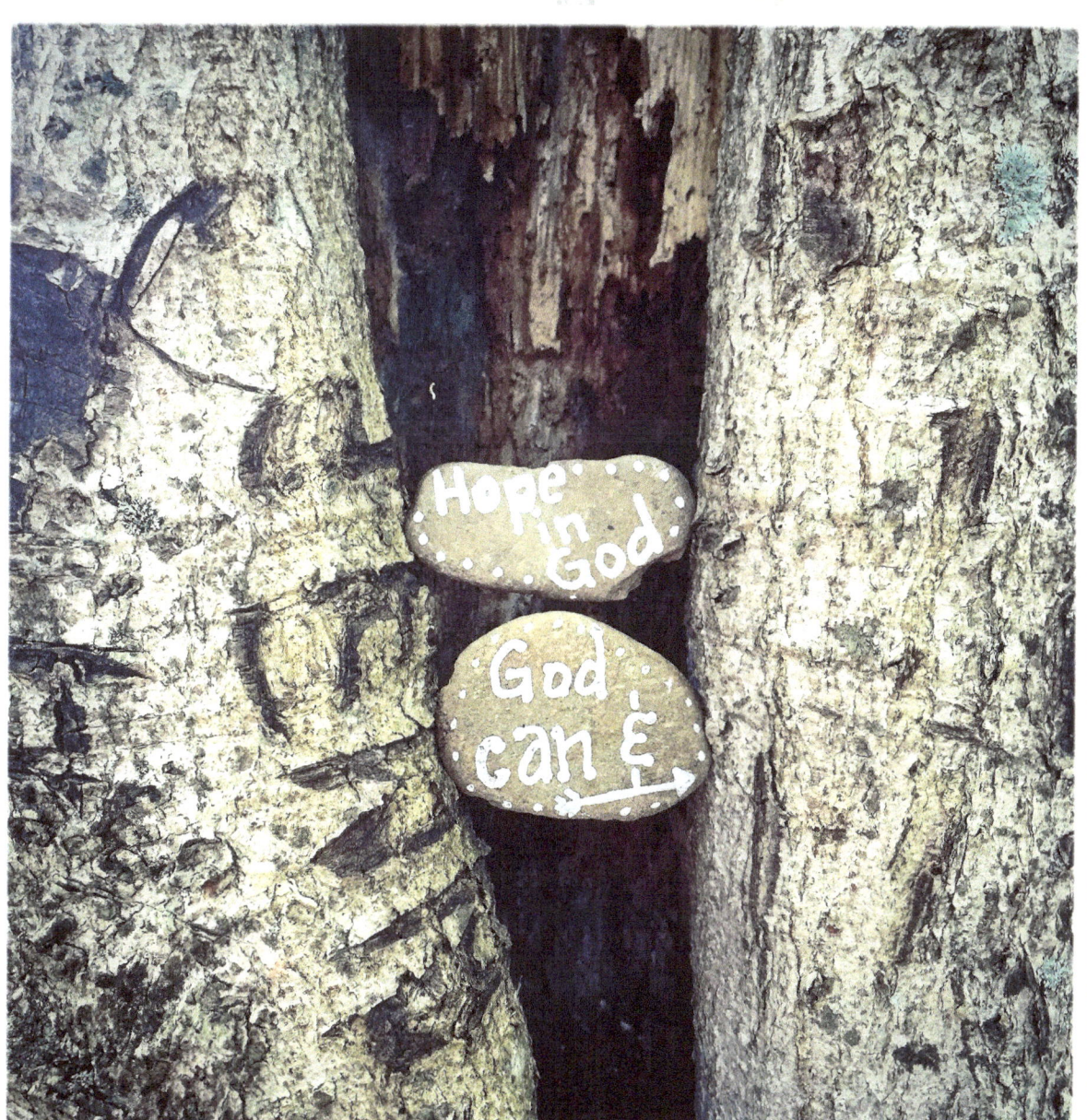

journaling questions

"ASKING QUESTIONS IS OF INESTIMABLE IMPORTANCE"

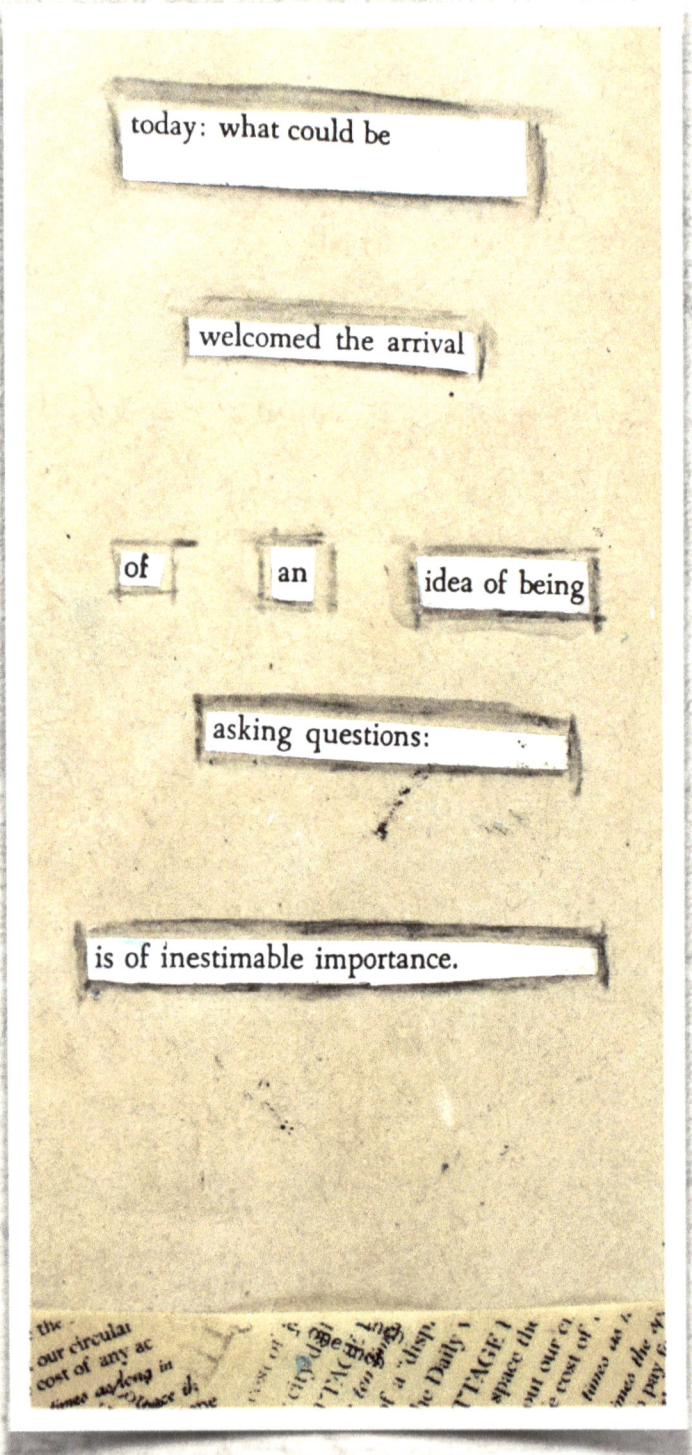

today: what could be

welcomed the arrival

of an idea of being

asking questions:

is of inestimable importance.

Based on the fact that you are the one in charge of the setting of your heart, let's do a reset. Let's go higher, by comparing your present situation with what is possible:

_____
_____
_____
_____
_____
_____
_____

God is always up to a "new thing". The arrival of the next new thing is always pending. What is one more thing you need to welcome into your life? (Do not write about what needs to go…write about what you want ushered in!)

_____
_____
_____
_____
_____
_____
_____

Your initiative is also your gift to God. It is your unique way of seeing. It is a fresh idea of being in the world. Choose one more thing you want to do differently, and write about it:

_____
_____
_____
_____
_____
_____
_____

There are a few people I need to thank
for their inspiration and input into this project:

First, my daughter Hannah, for tossing
this whole idea at me in the first place. Brilliant.   I love
you.

My daughter Sarah, for being my biggest cheerleader - and for
understanding why mama couldn't come out and play all those days.
I love you!

Next, I have to thank Ann Barton (aka "MomAnn").
Without you, my whole family would not be
where it is today. You love well.

My friend Delana B. (aka Delana Buyck) ~
Our lunch that day in 2012 changed my life. Thank you for
encouraging me to ignore my misplaced urges to fill out job
applications or join multi-level marketing companies. I have
filled my empty nest hours with a creativity that has been
unleashed by the grace of God.
(And the afternoons I get to spend in your's and Tim B's jeep have
helped keep that creativity happy and alive.)
I owe you, sis.

Lastly, thank you Jeanne Oliver.
We found each other when I was coming up out of a pit.
I was clawing my way into a new season,
and you made me feel seen and heard.
Our friendship has been sheer delight,
and when you asked me to write "Salt and Light"
for your network,
a light turned on in my heart.

The very day I emailed the finished version of the devotional
"Salt and Light" to you. . .

. . .I poured myself a strong cup of coffee. . .

and began writing "The Women of Advent".

This book would not have happened without you, and Salt and Light.
Literally.

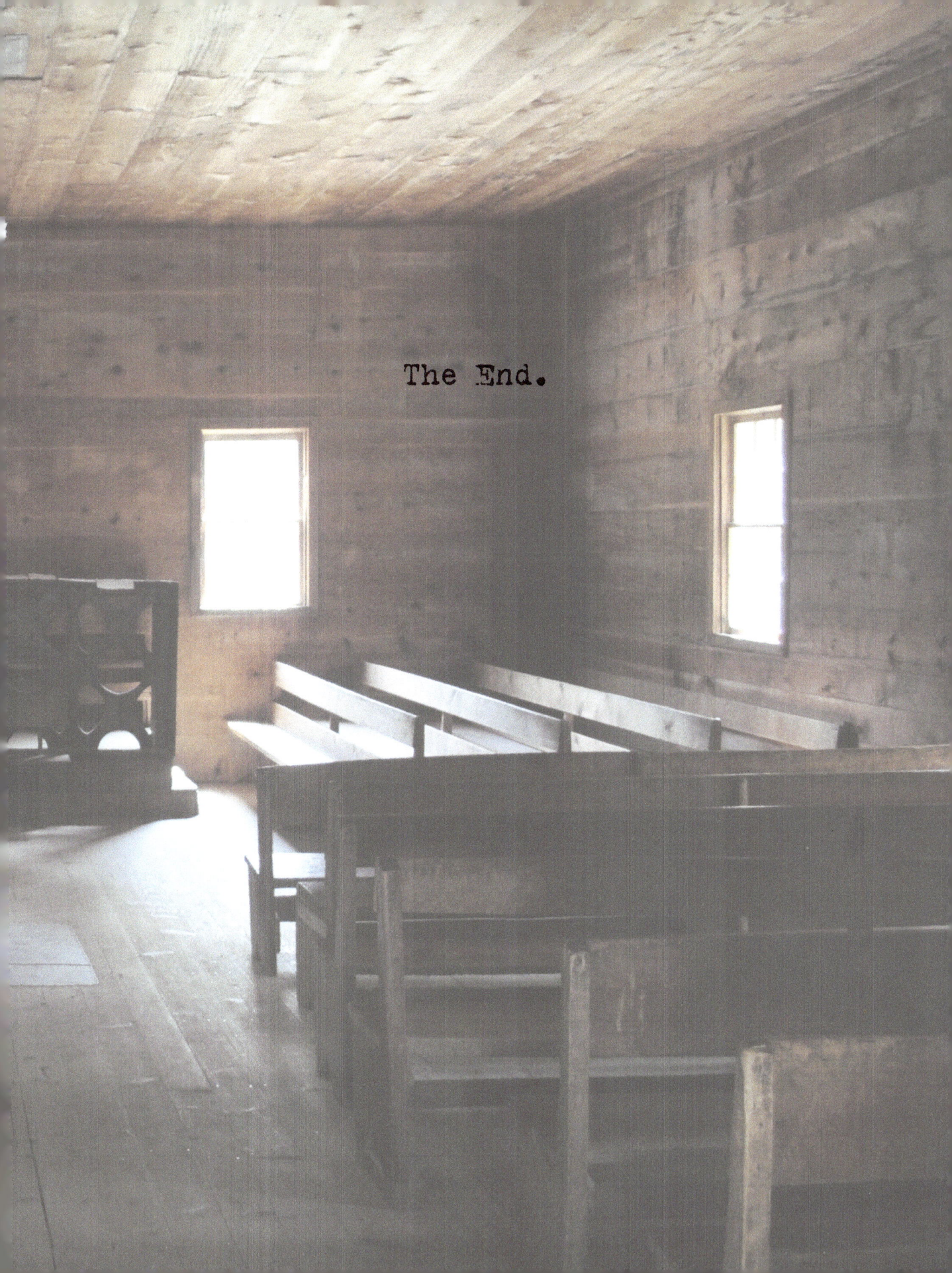

The End.

www.ingramcontent.com/pod-product-compliance
Lightning Source LLC
Chambersburg PA
CBHW050850180526
45159CB00007B/2629